Petals of

Love

Chronicles of The

Imperfectly Perfect Mother

Curated by:

Dr. Tiesha N. Bryant

Journey Through the Garden

Acknowledgements

"Your unwavering love and support have carried me."

God, I thank You for it all. Thank You for not only allowing me to birth and raise a child in the natural—but for also giving me the honor of birthing purpose.

To my Beautiful Petals, thank you for seeing my vision, knowing my heart, and understanding the assignment. This is BIG—and without you, it wouldn't be possible.

To the women in my life, thank you for loving me and showing me the way. Your unwavering love and support have carried me.

To my Mother-in-love, Ms. Denise Bryant, thank you for editing this project with such care and excellence. I know your motherhood journey is one marked by both great trials and triumphs.

I'm so blessed to be part of your legacy—because you birthed and raised such a loving, strong, and finnneeee (yes, I said it! lol) son. The one I'm blessed to call husbae.

To my Teemommy, my spiritual advisor, Apostle Dr. Shalonda "Treasure" Williams Lynard, thank you for saying yes to writing the foreword, even while working on your own powerful project, *"Love as the Master Healer: A Spiritsoulistic Journey To Wholeness"* Your wisdom, covering, and unwavering support mean the world.

To my coach, Charmain Stephens, thank you for seeing the vision, challenging me with love, and helping me pull this out of the depths of my soul. You are more than a coach; you are a gift.

To my daughter, Tanaya, Momma loves you really big. I'm so proud of you, baby girl. Thank you for your grace and unconditional love.

You've taught me so much on this journey—and you're still teaching me. I didn't want you to leave… not because you weren't ready for the world, but because I wasn't ready to let you go.

But look out world—she's grown now, and she's a force to be reckoned with. My prayer remains: God's protection, prosperity, and peace be your portion. Continue to soar, princess. Momma is so proud of you.

To my son, Tyshaun, I miss you real bad. I find myself looking back at our old messages.

I remember asking you if it was okay for me to share you with the world, given the platform I was on and the reach God was giving me… and you said yes.

I haven't stopped sharing—and I never will. I'll always remember your grocery list. Your music playlist. Even the last thing I bought you—books.

My heart aches that you're no longer here with us, but I know your spirit lives on. You're free now. I love you, son. (儿子)

To my Mother, Tracey, the motherless child who raised three beautiful daughters, helped raise a son, and nurtured four grandkids. You have mothered many. You did your big one, mama!

Thank you for your love, your nurturing spirit, and your example.

To my father, David, thank you for forgiving me. Thank you for your provision and for loving me.

Your hard work and love never goes unnoticed.

To my husband, Tjai, thank you for giving me the opportunity to be a boy mom, even if just for a little while, it made a lifelong impression.

Thank you for bringing balance to my motherhood journey. I love you.

To my village, I love y'all. Thank you for being part of my journey, my strength, my anchor, my reminder that I never have to do this alone.

To every Mother, near and far, I love you. This book is for you. It is your mirror. Your reminder. Your gentle nudge.

Welcome to... The Petals of Love. Los Pétalos del Amor. Na Duilleagan Gràidh

To my Petals who were picked from my garden, I miss y'all oh so much. You came to my rescue on this journey called motherhood. You were my rock, my escape, and my mouthpiece.

The garden you're in now is so much more beautiful. Continue to watch over me, just as you always have.

This is my thank you and my tribute to you.

Rest peacefully, Auntie Barbara Upshaw and
my God Momma Alberta Jackson.

Foreword

"Dr. Tiesha has gathered a beautiful array of women… who share messages of hope, encouragement, and empowerment…"

Dr. Shalonda "Nspirtational Treasure" Williams-Lynard

As an author and co-author of over twenty books to date, I believe that projects done with heart and purpose carry a healing energy just waiting to be encountered. However, while being asked to contribute to such a worthy project takes trust, agreeing to do it takes courage every single time. And that's not something that always comes easy. Oftentimes, it is a wild inner battle that ensues before courage wins out.

The inner tug-of-war between courage and low self-worth is what happens, and it is real. During the moments of contending, every word that has ever provoked a sense worthlessness within seems to come out and play. The messages of life that have been so confusing at times may cause one to forget that their divine value always has and always will be. Not just as a contributor to this powerful work, but as a mother as well.

I spent years questioning my value as a mom. I carried and birthed six biological children, and I still have moments when I rock myself to sleep with thoughts of uncertainty and concern. Add to that all those I've been assigned to nurture in this lifetime - bonus children, spiritual children, godchildren, and those entrusted to me by their parents to assist in one way or another. One can only imagine the anxiety that can and has been induced. "Am I doing this right?" "Should I be more lenient or should I be more firm?" "Will they hate me forever for this 'no' I have to give them?" "When is it time to let them go so they can find their own path?" "Have my decisions scarred them beyond repair?"

Question after question... fear upon fear... uncertainty and more uncertainty... loss and gain. It all comes with motherhood and the authors in this book speak these truths.

Every author in this work, starting with the curator – who just so happens to be one of those spiritual daughters – has shared their truths of motherhood with sincerity and transparency. Dr. Tiesha has gathered a beautiful array of women from different backgrounds who share messages of hope, encouragement, and empowerment to remind you that you are not alone. They share because they remember their personal tug-of-wars. They share because they felt the pull to show up in strength for those who may feel discouraged, weakened or weary from life's happenstances. They showed up in this book to resonate and to say, "you are doing the best you can with what you have, just keep your head up."

As you read every word, know that you are not alone and you are celebrated. Let this work sprinkle *Petals of Love* right there next to your feet and when you are done, stand on them and be reminded that you are a blessed mother; in whatever way you intend to be.

Big hugs Loved One and many blessings,

Dr. Shalonda "Treasure" Williams-Lynard

Author of Love As The Master Healer: A Spiritsoulistic Journey to Wholeness

Introduction

"This anthology? It's bigger than me. It's bigger than you.
Honestly, it's so big, I can't even fully put it into words."

Hey y'all!

It's Dr. Tiesha N. Bryant from Pittsview, Alabama. Yes—*that* small town tucked in Russell County. We might be small, but baby, don't let that fool you—there are some amazing people who come from there.

This anthology? It's bigger than me. It's bigger than you. Honestly, it's *so big*, I can't even fully put it into words. What I *can* say is that this book is the beginning of someone's healing journey. Whether it's through a release or an embrace—healing is here.

Every story shared is an intimate piece of motherhood. The tears. The pain. The laughter. The prayers. The triumph. The *resilience*. You'll feel it ringing through every single page.

As parents, there's no true handbook to parenting— (I mean, **Imperfectly Perfect: Three Steps on the Parenthood Journey** by yours truly *is* a really good resource though—just saying!) But what this book *does* hold are real parents, real women, who understood the importance of healing while mothering.

Because the truth is: We must heal so our kids can live. When we're whole, we don't operate from hurt—we respond from love. Our reactions aren't trauma-fueled; they're rooted in truth, grace, and patience. This is your first time being your child's mother... and their first time being your child. So, extend grace. To them. To you.

This edition of *Petals of Love* is a gentle reminder: We all go through something. But there is always greatness on the other side—*as long as you keep going.*

Let these pages inspire you. Let them guide you. Let them remind you that even the messiest seasons can produce the most beautiful blooms. Just like the lotus flower—rising through mud and murky waters—we, too, rise. Not because life was easy, but because we chose to bloom anyway.

And, if you take nothing else from this book, remember this: We may be *imperfectly perfect*—but that simply means, we are perfect for our kids.

This is Petals of Love. A tribute to imperfectly perfect motherhood. A sacred gathering of women who dared to be vulnerable, to heal, and to share. It's more than a book, it's a movement. Let the healing begin. Let the blooming continue.

Dr. Tiesha N. Bryant
Pittsview Made, Purpose Led

Petals of

Love

A Journey of Resilience and Growth

"I was a motherless child, trying to figure out how to become the very thing I never truly had – a mother."

By Paris Graham

In 2001, at the age of sixteen, I became a mother. While most girls my age were figuring out high school and dreaming about prom dresses, I was trying to determine how I was going to raise a human being while trying to understand what it meant to be one myself. The fear that gripped me was not just about diapers and sleepless nights. It was something deeper. I was a motherless child, trying to figure out how to become the very thing I never truly had – a mother.

There's no manual for motherhood, but when you've never even seen one modeled up close, you're fumbling in the dark. I didn't know how to hold space for emotions I hadn't been allowed to express. I didn't know how to show up consistently when my own foundation had always felt cracked. And yet, there he was, this tiny, innocent being depending on me to figure it out. And so, I got busy with the job.

I learned one moment at a time. I learned how to listen, even when my own mind was screaming. I learned how to love without condition, even when I didn't always love myself. And I learned how to grow up quickly, because I had no other choice but to rise.

By 2005, I had three children. The weight of responsibility was heavy, but so was the warmth of their little arms around my neck. Life was a series of routines, sacrifices, and silent prayers.

I entered a marriage that was supposed to be my safe space, my shared shelter in the storm. But it wasn't. It became another battlefield, one filled with neglect, tension, and eventual abuse - the kind that doesn't just bruise the body but breaks the spirit instead.

Leaving wasn't easy, but when God opened that door, I quickly busted through it. There's no perfect time to leave the person that you once dreamed would be your one and only. However, I knew I had to not only save my babies, but I had to save myself. I walked away from the marriage, from the pain, and from the idea that surviving was enough. I didn't want to just survive. I wanted to thrive.

Single motherhood became my new reality. It was the kind that people whisper about with sympathy or judgment, never really understanding the grit it takes to hold everything together when you're the only one showing up. Poverty was real. Support was scarce. Some days, I felt like I was pouring from an empty cup, scraping together the last pieces of energy I had to attend basketball games, volleyball games, football games, gymnastic competitions, dance competitions, etc. My babies were busy, and their Mama was tired!

Through it all, we made it! We laughed. We danced in the kitchen. We cried. We were healed. My children watched me fall and rise again, time after time. They saw me make mistakes, apologize, and try harder day after day. They learned that love wasn't about perfection. It was about presence.

Then, in 2017, I welcomed my fourth child - a new chapter - a different kind of beginning. I was older, wiser, still healing, still growing, but more grounded than I'd ever been. This time, I mothered with intention and clarity that I didn't have at the age of sixteen. It was a chance to do things differently - not perfectly, but consciously.

Motherhood changed everything for me. It taught me the art of vulnerability, of letting people see me, not just in my strength, but in my weakness. I learned to ask for help, to let go of pride, and to release the need to have it all figured out. I learned that being *"strong"* didn't mean never breaking down. Sometimes, strength is choosing to get back up -

again and again, even when no one is watching. Never forget to check on your "*strong*" friends.

There were times I felt completely alone, but I was never without purpose. My children became my reason, my mirror, and my motivation. They pushed me to dream bigger, to heal my trauma, to build a life filled with love, intention, and stability. They saw the worst of me and still believed in the best of me!

Now, as my three children have stepped into adulthood, I see something remarkable - they have broken the generational curse! They communicate with compassion. They honor their emotions. They love with intention. I've watched them set healthy boundaries, challenge toxic cycles, and hold space for others in ways I never knew how to at their age. They are building lives with self-awareness, emotional intelligence, and peace.

They are not repeating what they came from. They're redefining it! They're making conscious choices rooted in healing, not survival. They are proof that love, resilience, and growth can rewrite history. I didn't just raise survivors. I raised cycle-breakers!

Through them, I see the legacy I prayed for - the kind that doesn't just echo pain, but instead, amplifies purpose. And that, to me, is the real triumph of motherhood!

Still Doing It All for You, Tiyari

A Mother's Faith, A Daughter's Legacy,

A Life Rebuilt in Purpose...

"She taught me just as much as I taught her. How to pause and notice the little things. How to love without holding back. How to be present".

By Trina Washington- Hawkins

From the moment she was born, she filled my life with color. Her laugh could part clouds, her presence lit up rooms, and her spirit brought peace to chaos. She was curious, loud in the most joyful way, wise beyond her age, and compassionate without limits. Whether we were on the road for a spontaneous trip, shopping like we had endless credit, or in church giving God His due - those moments were sacred to us. That was our rhythm. That was our bond.

Tiyari had a light that drew people in. She never met a stranger. If she saw you - even across a room - you were getting a loud *"Hey!"* and a full smile. She cared deeply for others, often placing their needs above her own. She was humble, but her spirit was bold. She joked, she surprised people, and she made everyone feel seen. Her joy was contagious and her energy unforgettable.

She taught me just as much as I taught her. How to pause and notice the little things. How to love without holding back. How to be present. Her wisdom showed up in how she loved, how she gave, and how she handled people with grace. She was the reason I did what I did, and she's still my *"why."*

Some of my favorite memories are tucked away in simple moments. She loved Atlanta, so we went often. Lenox Square Mall was her favorite. One time she asked if she could go look at clothes while I stepped away. When I walked into Neiman Marcus, there she was - standing on the platform, $400 jeans hugging her hips, a personal shopper doting on her like she was royalty. I said, *"If you don't hurry up and get your butt out of those jeans—you betta!"* We laughed all the way back to Mississippi. You couldn't tell her that her mama wasn't rich! She knew I'd get her anything - but she never really asked for much.

That's just who she was. I remember one Christmas when she kept saying she didn't want anything. I finally got her to say "socks," and not just regular ones - different socks. So, I bought her socks - and so did everybody else! She ended up with so many, some never even got worn. It's one of those small memories that still makes me smile.

Then came August 8. That morning began beautifully! We had taken family portraits, just me, her, and my husband. We had marriage counseling at church afterward, and my bridal party was planning to come by later to choose dresses. Tiyari was supposed to go back to the house ahead of us to help get things ready for the bridal party. But she never made it.

She was in a car accident on the way home. And she didn't survive her injuries.

In one breath, joy turned into devastation. Just hours earlier, we were smiling for photos, laughing about hairstyles and dresses. And now - she was gone. My baby - my whole world - never came back through that door.

At first, I moved on autopilot. My husband looked at me and said, *"You can't break down now. You still have to take care of the baby."* And as much as I didn't understand those words in that moment, I knew I had to keep going. That same week, I sat beside her beautician while she did her hair for the last time. And then I did her makeup - just like always. Who else was going to do it? That was my baby. I had done everything for her in life, and I wasn't about to stop now!

But after the funeral... after everyone left... that's when the grief came crashing down! The loss of my daughter was a shattering pain no words could ever fully explain. It felt like the world itself collapsed, leaving nothing but silence and an ache so heavy, I couldn't breathe. I didn't just lose my child - I lost a part of myself! Her laughter that once filled our home was replaced by a deafening stillness. Her room has stood untouched, sacred. I couldn't bring myself to change anything.

Grief didn't just visit me - it moved in! It wrapped around my chest and took the air from my lungs. Some days I couldn't get out of bed. Other days, I tried and failed. The pain was physical - my heart didn't just ache; it throbbed! I felt like a mother stripped of her role, like my identity had been rewritten in the worst way. And I broke - quietly, slowly - but I broke.

In that pit of despair, I reached for the only thing that had never failed me - my faith. I cried out to God, not asking "why?" but simply asking Him to hold me together! "Either make me okay or let me be with her," I told Him. I found refuge in His Word. Psalm 34:18 became my anchor: *"The Lord is close to the brokenhearted and saves those who are crushed in spirit."* And I was crushed. But I was not alone.

Little by little, I gave myself permission to grieve. To speak her name without apology. To cry when I needed to. To smile when a memory warmed my soul. I stopped pretending to be okay. I started trusting that her story wasn't over. Her legacy wasn't gone. It was just mine to carry forward now!

We scattered her ashes throughout the South - places she loved, places that held pieces of our journey. That was one of the hardest things I've ever done. But now, every time I travel, I feel her beside me. Her presence isn't gone - it's just different.

Sixteen years later, her room is still untouched. I'm not ready, and that's okay. There is no schedule for healing. I've learned that. I've also learned this: *I can keep going. I can turn pain into purpose!*

Today, I live out that purpose through my businesses. I am *The Business Educator*, teaching others how to build solid foundations. I run *Taxes by Trina*, helping families and business owners secure their futures. I manage *Washington Monument Properties*, building generational wealth and investing in the community. And with my husband, I co-own *Hawkeye Seasonings*, a brand that started in Yari's Snack Shop and now touches tables across the world. These aren't just businesses. They are legacy. Her legacy. Every move I make is rooted in the love we shared and the future she inspired.

She used to say, *"Mama, everybody don't think like you,"* and I'd shoot back, *"Well, they should!"* Then we'd laugh so hard it hurt. I still hear that laughter. It echoes through everything I do.

To every mother who has lost a child - your pain is real, and your story matters. Grief isn't the finish line. It's a path you walk with trembling steps and an unshakable heart. You are still a mother. You always will be. Speak their name. Share their story. Keep their light shining.

I'm still doing it all for you, Tiyari!
Always, Mama

Breaking Cycles,

So My Kids Can Bloom

"This chapter of my life is not about perfection. It is about persistence. It is about choosing to parent with presence even when I am triggered."

By Francine "Sistah Fran" Umaru

The quote that deeply resonates with my soul is, ***"When a flower doesn't bloom, you fix the environment in which it grows, not the flower"*** *a quote by Alexander Den Heijer.* Unfortunately, just like we do not get to choose our parents, growing up as children, we do not get to choose our environment. Whether it be the household or the community. Would you believe me if I told you that growing up, I had no choice but to learn how to advocate for myself? The environment that I was planted in was not conducive to my growth; however, God already had plans for me with a purpose that could have only been birthed from the pain of parental wounds, and that is where my passion stems from.

> *"My parents were not my advocates or protectors; they were the perpetrators."*

Do you know what that feels like growing up? I might as well have been adopted or in foster care because my parents were in no position to raise children. The physical and emotional neglect began in Philly, but the abuse began in North Jersey. It all started with the puberty talk, not with my mother but with my father. After that talk, the uncomfortability never stopped. It was the way he would look at me and little did I know that I was being groomed at that moment. What did that look like in the dysfunctional environment that I grew up in? First, let me define the term *"grooming."* It is a well thought out and strategic plan by the perpetrator to build rapport with the victim and gain their trust before they are targeted.

Unfortunately, it was during the grooming process when I lost my voice. This is why it is extremely important that we make it a priority to empower our kids by having the *"safe/unsafe touch and body boundary"* talk with them as early as possible. Since my mother did not have that talk with me, I was not empowered nor was I prepared. How do you even disclose or put into words that a parent violated your body? My father almost convinced me that it was completely normal, but little did I know that this was only the beginning of a cult-like and dysfunctional family system that I will fortunately escape before becoming an adult. There is no doubt that my mother was complicit because she was intentional about working nights and weekends. My father already had a history of abuse, which had already occurred with another sibling.

Parenting in Safe Spaces

Fast forward nearly two decades and here I am. As I celebrate and reflect on my 38th birthday this past April, I realize that just nineteen years ago, I became a mother. For the past nine years, I have been married to a man that is willing to help me unpack the burdens so I can lay them down with God. In our marriage, we have unpacked, unlearned and strived to understand each other through a trauma-informed lens.

Being a mother to two authentic and unapologetic children, Fatimah who is 8 years old and Jahvoni who is almost eighteen, helps me to see myself without the filters. I cannot hide my true self from them, that is the true beauty of motherhood. Our home is not perfect, but it is safe. It is filled with honest conversations and full transparency. My husband and I are still healing… every single day. The mother and father wounds that I am often reminded of run deep, and complex trauma does not vanish. It lingers, it whispers, it fights for attention, but I strive to heal, not only for myself, but so that my children can bloom into the human beings they were meant to become.

One of the biggest lessons that I have learned as a parent is that you must heal from your own stuff because if you do not, you will be adding to the baggage of your children. A wise woman once told me that our children will have baggage to carry whether we intend to or not and that there may be things that we have added to it unintentionally. However, my goal is that their baggage is not as heavy as mine and I have been intentional about lightening my own load.

I highly support giving my children a safe space to speak up and this may be a taboo topic for many cultured families, however, I would hate for my kids to struggle with speaking up and feeling validated when they become adults. Many adults, including adult survivors of childhood abuse, struggle with identity crisis because they were not given the space to be their authentic self as a child. When we speak of "safe spaces," we must not forget about our children and their personal development.

Community Versus Village

One of the hardest things that I had to come to terms with was that as a cycle breaker, it is a lonely road. After you make the courageous decision to *"speak up,"* please be prepared to lose the village that you were once a part of. Being a part of a community is crucial in your journey because you cannot be self-actualized without a sense of belonging, it is human nature. Join the organization, the club, the church, the sorority... especially one that shares your mission and values. The difference between a community and a village is that a village is more closely knit and intimate than a community. A village usually consists of the people in your inner circle, and it may change along with the seasons of your experience. The few people that I consider a village do not live in the DMV community near us and cannot show up for us in ways that we need sometimes, which is no fault of their own. Have you heard of the African Proverb, *"A child who is not embraced by the village will burn it down to feel its warmth?"* This is an insightful proverb about connection and community. I know for sure that God equipped me with the courage to speak up, but due to the family isolation He knew that I would experience, He blessed me with many community outlets. For cycle breakers like us, this is not optional, it is mandatory in order to thrive and bloom into our higher selves.

The same people who should have sheltered and surrounded me with support turned their backs on me because I spoke my truth. I spent years navigating motherhood struggling with unresolved trauma, mental health challenges, and the ever-lurking shadows of my childhood. So, my healing journey consists of trauma-informed therapy and reparenting myself. Being the cycle breaker does not always feel empowering. Sometimes, it feels lonely. My children have felt the weight from the absence of a village and the lack of support systems.

This chapter of my life is not about perfection. It is about persistence. It is about choosing to parent with presence even when I am triggered. It is also about creating emotional safety when I never knew what that looked like and showing my kids that healing is messy and brave. I did not have a map, but I forged a path. And though it is marked by pain, it is also blooming with purpose. I was never the flower that refused to bloom. I was the gardener rebuilding the soil, pulling the weeds, and planting seeds of safety, honesty, and love. The quote by Alexander Den

Heijer lives in my bones because it reminds me that I was never broken, just misplaced. And now, my children are growing up in an environment where they are nurtured, seen, and free.

God took what was meant to destroy me and turned it into something sacred. I was not given advocates, I became one. My voice, once silenced by shame, is now a light for my children and anyone else who needs permission to speak. This is what breaking cycles look like. This is what blooming feels like.

Built in the Fire:

A Mother's Journey to Redemption

"Motherhood didn't come to me gently—it came in a storm."

By Tiecia Ayers

At 19, I was a college dropout and a single mother, holding a newborn and wondering how I got there. I felt like a failure. The world had expected so much from me, and I didn't know how to face it with a baby in my arms and nothing in my name. But even then, in my emptiness, I was carrying purpose. God knew the plan, even when I didn't.

From the second grade, I had been a caretaker. My father was away in the military for most of my life, and my mother—though doing her best—was consumed with survival. She was in the streets, clubbing and hustling, trying to keep us dressed and fed, but not emotionally available. So, I learned early on that if anything was going to get done, I had to do it. That included raising my younger brothers, cooking meals, and learning how to be a grown woman before I was even done being a little girl.

Still, I excelled in school. I became captain of the cheerleading team and graduated with honors. I had dreams. I wanted more. But then came love, or what I thought was love. Then came the pregnancy. Then came the shame. The bright future everyone saw in me dimmed behind judgment and disappointment.

In February of 2008, I was a teenager holding my newborn while being beaten by a man who claimed to love me. That moment broke me open. My uncle stepped in and put me and my son on a plane to Texas, where my mother had relocated. I arrived with two suitcases and a three-month-old baby. No plan. No peace. No safety net.

But I had him. And that was enough to start again.

I didn't have the blueprint for motherhood. I was learning as I went. I was parenting while healing from wounds I didn't even have the words for yet. But I loved my son deeply. I worked multiple jobs, enrolled in school, and failed more times than I can count. I cried. I prayed. I doubted myself. But I didn't quit—because he needed me. And I needed him more than he will ever know.

He gave my life structure. He gave my pain meaning. He gave my fight purpose. I built discipline because he needed stability. I rebuilt confidence because he deserved to see what a whole woman looked like. And slowly, I stopped surviving and started living.

By 2014, I earned my bachelor's degree—seven years after I started. That moment was more than a graduation; it was a declaration: I was becoming.

Then came law school. I studied, raised my son, and passed the bar exam on the first try. I thought finally—finally—I'd made it to the other side. But even after becoming a lawyer, life wasn't done humbling me.

In 2019, I found myself pregnant again. This time, I was already a single mother. The man who once supported me and my oldest son fell apart under the weight of life. What felt stable turned toxic. Verbal abuse. Emotional neglect. Another abandonment. Another storm. But this time, I was different. I wasn't that scared teenager anymore. I had built myself once, and I would do it again.

My second son was born during a pandemic—right in the middle of heartbreak, confusion, and fear. And yet, his presence brought peace. He reminded me that beauty can still show up in broken places. That hope doesn't ask for perfect timing, it arrives when it's needed most.

Raising two boys, twelve years apart, has shown me every side of myself. My oldest saw me struggle and rise. He saw me studying during his sleep hours, crying in silence, and still showing up. He is calm, kind, and a steady reflection of the survival years. My youngest gets a different version of me. One that has more freedom. More softness. More joy. He gets dance parties, field trips, bedtime stories, and the little things I missed the first time. They are both part of the same miracle: my transformation.

Motherhood didn't just teach me responsibility. It taught me resilience, reflection, and radical love. It taught me how to advocate fiercely, not just in courtrooms, but in life. My children gave me something no title or degree ever could—identity. They are my why. Everything I've built—my firm, my peace, my life—was built with them in mind.

In 2021, I launched The Law Office of Tiecia Ayers. Not because everything was finally perfect, but because I stopped waiting for someone else to validate me. I stopped tolerating mistreatment. I stopped hiding behind pain. I trusted God and built from the fire.

Today, my firm is flourishing. I advocate for those who feel unheard. I show up in the courtroom, and I show up at bedtime. I fight hard for justice, and I love even harder at home.

Motherhood saved me in ways I never expected. It forced me to grow up, show up, and rise above every label the world tried to stamp on me. It taught me that redemption is not a finish line, it's a daily decision to keep going.

I'm not perfect. But I am powerful.
I'm a mother. A lawyer. A survivor. A leader.
And my story is far from over.

Built from Broken,
Bossed Up Anyway

"They tried to bury us, but they didn't know we were seeds."

By Shavonne Schoolfield

Affirmations:

"I am not defined by my past, but by the power I found in my pain.
I am proof that broken pieces still build empires. I am resilient,
I am worthy, and I was born to rise."

Let me just say this up front - I didn't grow up thinking I'd be a mom at the age of fifteen. I was a baby having a baby. When my second son arrived, I was busy accumulating baby wipes while most girls my age were choosing their prom dresses.

I had to quit school in the 9th grade - not because I wasn't smart enough, but because I didn't have the support I needed. There were no parents in the stands, no one waking me up for school each morning, no help with diapers or late-night cries. It was just me, trying to make it one day at a time.

"Sometimes, the people you expect to catch you are the ones
who let you fall. You have to catch yourself anyway."

Their father? Let's just say he came with his own storms - physically abusive, emotionally damaging, and toxic from the inside out. I finally walked away bruised, broken, but not beat.

At the age of eighteen, I've slept on floors. I've fed my kids while I've gone hungry. I've held back tears in job interviews. I've shown up to school events looking like I had it all together when my world was falling apart. But I made a promise to myself that I would never let where I started be the place where I finished.

"I didn't come this far to only come this far."

I've tried nursing. I thought I could make a good living there until I realized the challenge. I felt anxiety just looking at a needle. So, boom, pivot!

I found a job building wire harnesses for aircrafts, and I was good at it. That opened a whole new door for me. I went to college and became an electrical engineer. That led me to a 25-year career in aviation. A Black woman, in a male-dominated industry.

"When one door closes, build your own entrance—
with hinges, bolts, and a business license."

But here's the kicker: I never let the hustle make me miss being a mom! I was still showing up at games, pushing education, clapping the loudest, and making sure my boys knew - even when the world didn't love them like I did - I always would.

Now? I own three successful businesses. My sons are thriving – educated, grounded and full of purpose.

"Strong women raise strong kids - even when
they're tired, broke, and healing in silence."

See, the moral of my story isn't just survival. It's transformation. It's about rewriting your story with whatever pen life puts in your hand - even if it's broken.

"Life might knock you down, but faith and hustle
will help you build from your knees."

So, to every young mom reading this, wondering if you've got what it takes - girl, you do! You are the plot twist. You are the comeback. And you are exactly what strength looks like in heels, sneakers, or barefoot on the kitchen floor feeding your baby with one hand and wiping your tears with the other!

Closing Affirmation:
"I am not what I've been through - I am what I've overcome. I choose purpose over pain, peace over pity, and power over my past. I am the proof that healing is real, and success is still mine."

Complete Grace

"Even in the heartbreak, I saw God's hand. I saw Him open doors that no one could shut."

By Dr. Sarah Grace

I can still remember sitting on the wooden slab steps that led down into the basement - the place we now called home. It was in Baltimore, the city I had returned to after my divorce, searching for stability and maybe a fresh sense of self. But nothing could have prepared me for the humility of that moment.

All seven of my children were sleeping on donated air mattresses scattered across the basement floor. And there I was - now a former full-time pastor, a homeschool mom, once living in the suburbs with two SUVs and a full ministry life - now quietly crying out to God on those cold wooden steps, asking, *"How did we get here?"*

Not too long ago, we had been doing ministry together - my husband and I - preaching, baptizing, building what we thought was a legacy. We had been ordained together. Baptized together. We even pastored together. Never in a million years did I imagine I would end up raising our children alone.

But the way life works sometimes - we make our plans, but life's decisions rewrite them. And even more importantly, God always has a way of taking our brokenness and rewriting it into beauty.

My first child was born out of wedlock. And though that chapter began with shame in the eyes of others, it was the very beginning of my walk with Christ. That baby brought me to my knees in a way that awakened my soul. And when I later married his father, and we went on to have six more children together, I believed I had finally found my *"forever."*

But forever doesn't always look the way we pictured. After years of trying, praying, counseling, and enduring, I made the hardest decision of my life - to walk away. It shocked everyone, including me. But I was determined to give my children peace, and to protect my own heart for the first time in a long time.

Even in the heartbreak, I saw God's hand. I saw Him open doors that no one could shut. I saw Him provide for our needs in supernatural ways - from people sponsoring summer camps and artistic programs, to my children being invited to act in Christian films, appear in magazines, and even walk red carpets.

I didn't orchestrate any of that. I couldn't have. I didn't have the means. But God's grace made room for our family in ways that can only be explained by heaven's favor.

There were many nights I cried. Many days I felt like I wasn't enough. I battled depression, doubt, and deep feelings of inadequacy. I lost my temper more times than I want to admit. There were moments my children saw me fall short - in parenting, in relationships, in faith. And yet, I learned how to be honest with them. I learned how to say, *"I'm still growing too."* I learned how to apologize and ask for grace, and how to model what it means to let God father me while I was trying to mother them.

Because as much as they were my babies… I was God's baby too.

One of the things I'm most grateful for is how God taught us, as a family, to value moments over materials. We didn't have much, but we had each other. Some of our best memories were movie nights in the living room, where we'd make popcorn, pull out all the blankets, and laugh until we cried. We'd have long family dinners where each child could talk about their day or what was on their heart. Birthdays were special - not because of expensive gifts, but because we celebrated each other with intentional love, words, and sometimes homemade cakes and decorations.

Those little things became everything. And somehow, through all of that, God gave me the grace to keep doing ministry - just in a new way. I wasn't pastoring anymore, but I was traveling and speaking. I would often take all seven of my children with me to churches or conferences. I'd line them up in a row before I preached, and they'd lay hands on me and pray before I walked to the pulpit. They sat through long services and late-night altar calls, showing patience and quiet strength far beyond their years. In those same years, I also wrote books and launched a television ministry. All while homeschooling, healing, and trying to keep a home together. It wasn't easy. But it was possible - not because of me, but because God was in the midst of it all.

"But He said to me, 'My grace is sufficient for you, for my power is made perfect in weakness.'"

- 2 Corinthians 12:9

Years later, I found myself sitting on another set of wooden slabs - but this time they formed the back porch of a peaceful home in rural Alabama. We had been given the use of four acres of land and lived there for nearly five years with very few expenses. That back porch became a sanctuary. A holy ground of sorts. I would sit and look out over the land and remember those basement days - not with bitterness, but with wonder at how far God had brought us. We have since relocated and God is providing another way but we will never forget our time of refuge in the mountains.

What was once a cry of *"How did we get here?"* became a song of *"Thank You, Lord, for bringing us through."*

And now, almost all of my children are grown. I have two teen-agers left at home, and I cherish every moment. Looking back, I don't see a perfect mother - I see a present one. One who didn't give up. One who tried, prayed, failed, learned, and kept showing up.

If you are reading this and you are in your own basement season - I want you to know this:

God sees you.
He hears the prayers you whisper in the dark.
And He has a plan - not just to rescue you,
But to redeem your story in ways that will blow your mind.

You don't have to be perfect. You don't have to be everything. You just have to lean on the One who is. Whether you're married, single, divorced, or widowed - God is the only perfect parent. We are simply vessels. Let's point our children to the One who never fails.

"The Lord will perfect that which concerns me..."
- Psalm 138:8

"A man's heart plans his way, but the Lord directs his steps."
- Proverbs 16:9

Live Intentionally
(NO INTERRUPTIONS)
"I had to go deep,
That trauma, them feelings,
that hatred and tension."

By Jasmine The Journeylist

I started living intentionally
It's really meant for me
Finna try the music industry
About to blow this thing up spiritually
the rose that growz
Keeping people on their toez.
You know why?
My story's poetic
Justice like Tupac
And Janet Jackson
I can do this by myself
Keeping God first,
creating generational wealth.
I had to go deep,
That trauma, them feelings,
that hatred and tension.
From my head down to my feet
Healing chakras yes indeed
No talk, just action
Like the law of attraction
Just like Aladdin,
That's when the magic happened…
God opened those doors for me
And went to war
Ain't let the enemy take control of me
Looking like a diamond
I know you see me, shining
With my husband right behind me.
He's so supportive
And he adores me
Never try to control me
Respect is there a stayed
I'm so damn glad I prayed
Thanking God for better dayz.
Respect is there it stayed,

Respect is there it stayed,
Respect is there it stayed,
Thanking God for better dayz.
My focused just increased,
I'm so freaking Unique,
Fabulous, aye
That life you want,
You've gotta go after it,
Can't be no hobby
You've gotta have passion widdit,
In everything you do,
You better self master it,
I'm so fly, and I'm so different
And I'm from the country, yep,
Cleveland, Mississippi
That means wonder bread and no tissue,
Two beds and a kitchen,
Grandma earned an honest living,
And took care of her kid's children
That's a different type of feeling,
You feel me? I'm cutting through the ego,
Getting down to the real me.
That's why I started…
Living intentionally
It's really meant for me
Finna try the music industry
About to blow this thing up spiritually
The rose that growz
Keeping people on their toez.

From Thirteen to Thirty-Three:

I Am

"But in that silence is where I met me! I heard God whisper, 'You are not broken. You are blooming!'"

By Dr. Tiesha N. Bryant

I became a mother by pregnancy, at age thirteen. I turned fourteen in March 2005 and gave birth September 22, 2005. Still a child - still figuring out who I was - and suddenly, I was responsible for someone else.

They whispered. Family included. "She's fast." "She ain't going to graduate." "She don't even know who that baby's daddy is."

But I wasn't fast. I was a church girl. A nerd. A family-first, kind-hearted, homework-loving kid. But life? Life doesn't ask for permission. It doesn't follow rules. It shifts you - suddenly, permanently - into places you never imagined standing in. And ready or not... I became a mother. Scared. Ashamed. Overwhelmed. But also wrapped in a love I didn't know could exist.

And thank God, literally, for my village. My mama. My aunties. My sisters. My best friend. My women. They didn't discard me - they covered me. My dad eventually got on board. In prayer. In encouragement. In wisdom.

My mom said, *"I got your back. Forget what the people say."* My aunts joined in, *"You ain't the first and won't be the last, you will still go to school and do what you got to do."* So, I did.

I fixed bottles while taking a break from doing my Algebra work. I held flashcards in one hand and my daughter in the other.

I graduated in the top 10% of my class when *"they"* said I wouldn't graduate at all - because failure was never an option. Because I had something to prove - not just to the world, but to myself!

So, I kept going. Honorary Doctorate. Licensed Master Social Worker. Certified Global Leader. Non-profit founder. Business owner, Speaker, and Coach. Every title was earned. Every step was fought for.

But if I'm honest... I wasn't just building a future - I was *running from my past*. Working hard was how I coped. The hustle was my hiding place. I didn't want my parents to ever feel ashamed. I didn't want my daughter to think her beginning would define her ending.

So, I went hard. I wore strength like armor. It wasn't until grief broke me open that I realized I was exhausted from proving I was enough. After we lost my bonus son in March 2024, I couldn't keep pushing like nothing happened. So, I sat down - with a therapist. I got still - with God. And I got real - with myself.

My spiritual mom looked me in the eye and said, *"Baby, your hustle is a trauma response. You've been proving yourself to people who already love you. It's time to prove it to you."*

Whew! That hit my soul like a mirror. Now I grind differently. Not from lack - but from legacy. Because before that grief... there was *love*. Love that came through bonus motherhood. And let me be clear - *blended families are not TV sitcoms*. They're complex. They're real. They're beautiful and broken and sacred all at once!

I married a man of discipline. Structure. Integrity. Accountability. He didn't bend easily - but he showed up strong! And I needed that. But I was still growing. Because remember - I was still a child raising a child. So, when our worlds collided - his way, my way, our wounds, our child - It got hard!

The rhythm of our home shifted. My daughter and I had to adjust to new rules, new energy, new love. There were moments we misunderstood each other. There were others that I questioned myself as a mom and a wife. But when I surrendered our family to God, the real blending began! Not just people in the same house - but hearts learning to live in unity. My husband and I? We became a team. Not perfect. But perfectly positioned for our babies.

And then came March 2024. We lost my bonus son. Suddenly. Painfully. Unbearably. The hardest part for me, in this great loss, was reminding myself that I had the right to grieve. That I wasn't *"just the wife."* That he was my son, too. I loved him. Prayed over him. Showed up for him. I had to mourn *my* baby too.

But grief didn't stop time. That same year, our daughter had prom, graduation, and college. So, I cried in secret and smiled in public. I zipped up dresses while my heart was breaking. I clapped at ceremonies while my soul was aching. I mothered in motion, very proud of her accomplishments, while grieving in silence.

Then August came, and she left for college. I became an empty nester and a grieving mother at thirty-three. The silence in our home echoed in ways I never expected. It was the kind of quiet that forces you to face everything you've been too busy to face before. But in that silence is where I met me! I heard God whisper, *"You are not broken. You are blooming!"*

Every title I've worn - from teen mom to bonus mom to wife to griever to healer - They are not my chains. They are my *petals!* Each one is proof that I was still growing. And now? I no longer hustle to prove. I rise to become.

So, if you ask who I am?

I am the girl who gave birth at the age of thirteen,
The woman who released and grieved at thirty-three,
The bonus mom who loved fiercely through conflict and loss,

The wife who had to grow into her role,

The mother who never stopped showing up,

Even when life tried to shut her down.

I Am...

Still healing.

Still stretching.

Still believing.

Still blooming.

I don't just carry petals of love - I am one.

I owe it all to God. And I am thankful for it all.

From Broken to Built

"I did not just survive those storms. I learned how to dance in the rain!"

By Dr. Shakea Miller

> *"Many are the plans in a person's heart, but it is the Lord's purpose*
> *that prevails."*
> *Proverbs 19:21*

I was nineteen when life shifted. Pregnant, confused, and newly withdrawn from college, I could hear the whispers around me loud and clear: *"She ruined her future."* What they did not know was that God was just getting started.

Being a teen mom is like walking into a storm without shelter. I was blessed to have a baby shower, but even with that celebration, I still felt the sting of judgment. The excitement was short-lived and replaced quickly with shame and silence from others. People treated my pregnancy like a tragedy, and if I am honest, for a while, I believed them. But what they saw as an ending, God saw as a beginning.

I pressed on through tears and sleepless nights, determined to make something of myself for my son. I enrolled in a trade school and became a certified nursing assistant. That decision opened doors. I pursued additional certifications in phlebotomy and clinical medical assisting. I was slowly rebuilding what I thought I had lost, but now with purpose.

I stayed in what the older generation called a *"shacking up"* situation, trying to raise my son in what felt like a two-parent home. Financially, we were stable, but emotionally, the relationship left me depleted. Eventually, I had to choose self-respect over comfort. I left. I moved everything into storage and began my new life as a single mother. Life became a roller coaster. I worked two jobs and leaned on my family when I could.

I met my now-husband when I least expected it, an old friend from high school who messaged me out of the blue. That message changed my life. He stepped up, not just for me, but for my son as well. After a heartfelt conversation where I laid out my needs and hopes, he asked me to marry him three months later. I said *"Yes!"*

We were married in March 2012, but the transition was not easy. He was an ex-felon, struggling to find steady work. I worked part-time while pursuing college online. Eventually, he was laid off, and I had no child support coming in. We struggled. We lost our home. For a time, we were homeless, sleeping in run-down hotels. It was the lowest I had felt in years. But just when it seemed we had hit rock bottom, God stepped in! In a miraculous turn, I received a call from the Tallassee Housing Authority. My Section 8 application from years earlier had finally come through! We moved into our new place with grateful hearts and renewed hope. Shortly after, I found work as a car salesperson.

Just as things were settling, I received life-altering news that I had cancer. Surgery was necessary, but thankfully, they removed everything! That experience reminded me of the fragility of life and the power of purpose. I made a vow that I would build something lasting, something that belonged to me.

With money from the car lot, I launched a tax business and a food truck. My first season was a success. Then came a new vision - a staffing agency. In 2016, I launched 1-On-1 Staffing, followed by a wellness clinic in LaGrange, Georgia, in 2017. That same year, I saw my first million in business! In 2018, we bought our first home. From Section 8 to a home of our own, God had truly turned it around!

In 2019, I launched 1-On-1 Technical College. I did not just want to create income; I wanted to create impact. After years of pouring into the community, in July 2024, I transformed my trade school into a two-year, post-secondary degree-granting institution and Theological college. This was not only a dream fulfilled, but also a historic milestone, as I became the first African American woman in Alabama to open such an institution.

That same year, I was accepted into law school, an accomplishment that represented more than academic success. It was a full-circle moment that proved no matter how far off-track life may seem, God's purpose always prevails!

In November 2024, I earned my Associate's Degree. In February 2025, I received my Bachelor's Degree, further solidifying my belief that it is never too late to reclaim your future. In 2024, I received three honorary Doctorate Degrees for my contributions to education, empowerment, and community transformation. I was also honored with two Presidential Lifetime Achievement Awards, one in 2023 and another in 2024. I was also published in the Black Enterprise Magazine, Troy University online article, along with many others. These were more than just accolades - they were divine confirmations that every struggle served a purpose!

My journey is also rooted in service. I now proudly serve as the Second Vice President of the local NAACP chapter, using my voice and platform to fight for justice, equality, and opportunity. I advocate fiercely for educational access and economic empowerment, because I have lived through the barriers and know the power of breaking them. Each title I hold - wife, mother, entrepreneur, dean, or advocate, carries the weight of every sleepless night, every doubtful whisper, and every storm I walked through. I did not just survive those storms. I learned how to dance in the rain!

To the mother reading this who feels overwhelmed, overlooked, or underestimated, you are not alone. God sees you. He is crafting a story that only you can write. Do not despise your detours. Sometimes, they are the very roads that lead to destiny.

Isaiah 61:3 says, *"He gives beauty for ashes, the oil of joy for mourning, and a garment of praise for the spirit of heaviness."* My life is living proof of that promise. What was meant to break me, built me. What was meant to shame me, shaped me. My story is not perfect. My path was not easy. But every step was necessary to get me here.

If you ever doubt whether God can use your brokenness, proof is on this page. He can. He will. And when He does, it will be more beautiful than you ever imagined.

Heaven Doesn't Have a Phone,

But God Still Hears Me

"I was seeking unconditional love, a connection that would fill the void and tether me to something greater than pain."

By Ashley Stringfellow

At thirty years old, I sat alone in tears, overwhelmed by the weight of infertility and unanswered prayers. I couldn't understand how some people were given the gift of motherhood, only to neglect their children or give them away, while I, someone longing to love deeply and completely, remained empty-handed. I asked myself, *"Why not me? Was I undeserving? Was God trying to show me that motherhood wasn't in His plan for my life?"*

The silence from heaven felt unbearable. Though I reminded myself that God would never place more on me than I could bear, I couldn't help but feel hopeless and inadequate. I cried out to Him, begging, pleading, aching to be a mother - not just to hold a child, but to heal the part of me that was shattered when I lost my own mother. I was seeking unconditional love, a connection that would fill the void and tether me to something greater than pain.

Motherhood had always been in my heart. I used to say, *"When I turn 30, I'll have my first baby."* But 30 came and went, and instead of joy, I was met with sorrow. For five years, I tried to conceive. Not once did I see two pink lines. Not even did I get a false positive to toy with my hope – just empty tests and emptier arms.

PCOS (Polycystic Ovary Syndrome) ravaged my body like a thief in the night. My hormones were a mess! My periods lasted for weeks at a time. The cysts on my ovaries stole my ability to ovulate. There were moments I didn't even feel like a woman. I was dealing with facial hair, weight gain, acne scars, and a body that seemed to betray me at every turn.

Weight had always been a battle. Since I was eleven, I had tried every diet, every cleanse, every fast to chase some unreachable ideal. I had prayed, punished, and pushed myself, only to feel like I was always failing. But during the pandemic, after waiting over a year, I finally had VSG (Vertical Sleeve Gastrectomy) surgery. It was my last hope! And slowly, the weight came off. My body felt like it was finally working with me. I lost over 80 pounds. And then by the grace of God, I conceived! No fertility treatments. No interventions. Just divine timing!

I was thirty-two years old and pregnant for the first time. I kept it quiet partly out of fear, partly due to job insecurity, and partly because I felt it was too sacred to share it too soon. On the outside, I was functioning. But on the inside, I was struggling. Depression didn't look like staying in bed all day. It seemed like I was doing everything necessary while feeling like I was doing nothing right. Postpartum crept in slowly, quietly, and my child's father didn't understand. He showed up financially, but I often felt emotionally and physically alone. Everyone brought gifts and baby clothes, but I needed sleep. I needed support. I needed someone to hold me while I held my baby.

Motherhood was a blessing, but also a shock. I didn't expect the isolation I experienced. I didn't expect the eventual guilt. I didn't expect to feel like an imposter. There were nights when my baby cried, and I had done it all, fed her, changed her, burped her and still, she cried. And I cried with her. That's when I missed my mother the most!

I used to whisper, *"I wish heaven was just a phone call away. I wish my baby could have experienced the woman who raised me."* I really missed my mother, who worked long hours but still came home and cooked baked chicken with rice and gravy. She taught me and my brother to wash our clothes, cook our meals, and take care of our home at an early age. We were *"latchkey kids,"* but we were never unloved. I remember her once saying, *"Y'all are smarter than me."* It wasn't shame. It was pride. She wanted more for us, and now I want the same for my daughter.

Help came in the form of someone unexpected, her auntie, but not by blood. She stepped in like an answered prayer. During the week, my daughter stayed with her. I received her help on the weekends. I sometimes joked that she was the *"baby mama"* and I was the *"baby daddy."* Unconventional? Yes, but it worked. Her home became a neutral, peaceful place where my baby's father could visit. It gave me time to work, to study, to breathe. Her auntie didn't just babysit. She built a bridge for my healing. She's family now, a blessing in my life.

I see my daughter throughout the week, and I never feel guilty about it. I know she is loved, safe, and surrounded by joy. She has bonus siblings to bicker with and play with, to follow around and learn from. And I do my part to pour back into our village, whether it's showing up for family dinners or letting her daughter practice makeup and lashes on me. Love is a loop, and I've learned to give and receive it more freely.

Through therapy and faith, I've learned one undeniable truth: You have to love yourself first. You cannot pour into your child from an empty vessel. You must become the example you want to set, but that can't happen if you're constantly depleted. And that can't happen without guidance from the Lord. God will order your steps. He will align people and moments you never imagined. You may not see the path clearly, but He is always working for your good.

I'm still learning, still growing, still becoming. But one thing I know without a doubt is this: My baby is loved. She is happy. She is healthy. And she is a daily reminder that even when heaven doesn't pick up the phone, God still hears me.

I Asked God For Five

"...the path may not look like the promise, but the promise still stands!"

By Chassidy Grady

I always said I wanted five children. Not four. Not six. Five. In my heart, I imagined the chaos of five little ones running around the house, all with my eyes, my husband's laugh, and our love woven into their DNA. I imagined them all coming from my womb - one by one - roof of a body that worked, a plan that unfolded perfectly, and a motherhood that matched my prayers. But life has a way of unfolding in the most unexpected - and most sacred - ways.

Over thirteen years ago, I married the love of my life and stepped into a ready-made family. I became an instant stepmother to three children - then ages five, four, and three. I wore the title proudly on the outside. On the inside, I was unraveling. I loved them deeply, but I also longed for a child I could carry - one whose first cry I'd hear, whose midnight feedings I'd endure, whose life I had carried inside of me.

There's a unique ache in feeling like a mother without the confirmation of birth. I silently questioned my worth. Was I strong enough? Did being a stepmother count? Could I embrace the gift before me while still yearning for what was missing?

In the years that followed, I battled infertility in silence. Two ectopic pregnancies left me heartbroken, confused, and angry. I wondered if God had skipped over me. Was I being punished? Was my dream of five just that - a dream?

Eventually, we turned to IVF (In Vitro Fertilization). I clung to hope as I underwent the process and God met me there. Our very first round was successful. We welcomed our son - my miracle boy - into the world. He reminded me that God still opens wombs and writes redemption stories.

Later, we hoped to grow our family again. But before we could begin another round of IVF, I became pregnant naturally - something I had been told was no longer possible. That pregnancy, too, ended as my third ectopic. It broke me in a new way. How could a miracle I wasn't supposed to have been taken away just as quickly? I grieved in silence. Still, I pressed forward, determined to try again.

Our next FET (Frozen Embryo Transfer) attempt failed. I wanted to cry, but I did not give myself permission to grieve at that moment. I was determined to not let go of the promise. So, we tried again. And God said "Yes!"

Our daughter - joyful, radiant, and full of life - came into the world and completed what I now see as a perfectly imperfect picture. She arrived not just to fulfill a dream, but to confirm that even after heartbreak, beauty can still be born! It was then that I remembered that I had asked God for *five!* And He gave me five, just not in the way I expected! Three children came through marriage. Two arrived through medical miracles. *Five children!* Just like I had asked.

Motherhood has taught me many things, but this truth stands above the rest: *the path may not look like the promise, but the promise still stands!* If I'm honest, I didn't always embrace that truth. I allowed shame to sit in the corners of my heart. There was shame for needing help to conceive. Then there was shame for struggling to bond in *"stepmotherhood."* Lastly, there was shame for feeling like an outsider in my own blended family. I believed the lie that I wasn't a real mother unless I had given birth. But healing came when I stopped striving and started surrendering. God met me in every broken place and whispered what grace always says:

"You are enough, even when you feel empty.
You are chosen, even when you feel skipped over.
You are a mother, no matter how your children come to you."

Today, I am the mother of five beautiful children - three through marriage and two through a journey marked by loss, faith, and resilience. I've learned that motherhood isn't about perfection - it's about presence. It's not about biology - it's about love. It's not about a straight path - it's about walking with grace through the winding roads.

To the woman in the waiting season - please don't give up. To the woman who feels ashamed of needing help to conceive - release that guilt. There is no shame on the route you take to meet your baby. To the woman who's struggling in stepmotherhood - give yourself compassion. Blending a family is holy and hard. You are doing better than you think. And to the woman who doubts if she'll ever hold a child in her arms - hold tight to this promise and do this:

"Delight yourself in the Lord, and He will give you the desires of your heart."
- Psalm 37:4

Sometimes the path to the promise is paved with pain - but the promise is still true.

Now I run a tax and bookkeeping firm while mothering five children in a blended, blessed, and beautiful family. Life is full, loud, layered - and absolutely divine! Some days, I still question if I'm doing this motherhood thing right. But I no longer question if I belong here. I do! And so do you! One of the affirmations that anchors me is this:

"God doesn't waste pain. He repurposes it."

Every loss, every tear, every long night of waiting - it led me here. To five children. To a healed heart. To a testimony I once didn't want to tell. We are all imperfectly perfect mothers. We carry hope in one hand and healing in the other. We love deeply, we pray constantly, and we keep showing up - even when the road is hard.

I asked God for five. And He gave me five - His way, in His time. And for that, I am forever grateful!

When the World Stopped,

We Started

"It's not about reinventing the wheel, traveling a large distance, or spending a ton of money."

By Jill Leman

When my husband, Matt, and I decided we were ready to start trying to have a baby, it was a well-thought-out decision. This was going to be our first child, and we had a lot of discussions to prepare. We had been together for years, married for one. Things were going well with our respective careers. The timing felt right. We are planners, so we did what we do best, and we made plans. But what was not a part of any of those plans? A worldwide pandemic!

Things were already shifting in New York City, where we lived, when I discovered the faint pink line on a stick. The city and the world were abuzz with panic and uncertainty. Within days of our big news, the city was on lockdown. The school where I taught and my husband's office moved to remote work for the foreseeable future. My own business, teaching in-person play classes and events in people's homes, stores, and play-spaces, had been growing and going well, but could no longer run as it had. Throughout the entire pregnancy, I tried very hard to focus on the positives and maintain a sense of humor about it all. At the end of the day, I was grateful to have a healthy pregnancy, and eventually a healthy baby.

But I think it's important to acknowledge what couples like us lost being first-time parents during this time. We couldn't share the excitement and celebrate with our friends and family in a normal way. With so many unknowns about how this virus affected pregnant women, we remained incredibly isolated throughout the entire pregnancy and a lot of my daughter's first year. Our friends and family were not with us through this… they didn't see my body change - as if this entire chunk of time, this major moment in our lives, just didn't exist!

My husband could not come to any appointments with me. He heard the baby's heartbeat for the first time on the phone, sitting in our parked car outside of my OBGYN's office. I'd Facetime him so he could see the blurry screen during my sonograms. But so much of his participation in the process was remotely from the car. This was particularly hard when we hit bumps in the road in the pregnancy, like when I had spotting at eleven weeks and had to make an emergency appointment to make sure we hadn't lost the baby or when my fluid levels dropped in my last weeks, moving up my delivery.

Obviously, I knew that becoming a parent was a huge responsibility that would involve making a lot of decisions and choices. But having to make these calls and ask ourselves *"Is this safe for my child?"* so often before she was even here... establishing our *"rules"* but not wanting to dictate what others are comfortable with, trying to navigate and make decisions in the name of her safety in a situation that was constantly evolving. It was so hard and so draining. What risks were worth taking? Which were not? The stakes felt so high. Because they were so high, I think this anxiety was formed during a lot of my early months, even years of parenting.

Ultimately, experiencing pregnancy and early motherhood in this way made me stronger. More resilient. The forced pivot in my career ended up being the best thing that could've happened, as it led me down the path that I'm on now. I started sharing simple play ideas on social media while everyone was spending so much time at home. Many of the brands I'd been running in-person store events for were looking for new and innovative ways to build a virtual community for their customers, and a whole new journey with my work began. It was one that allowed me to also be home with my daughter as the primary caretaker, with the flexibility to build my schedule around her needs and understand the parents I was supporting in a new and deeper way.

My daughter is now four, and I can say with confidence that being a mom is the most rewarding, impactful thing I've done in my life so far. I came into motherhood with a lot of knowledge and training about early development because of my work. And while coming into it with knowledge, tools, and expertise helps, I am still constantly learning.

My daughter is like a little mirror, and being her parent has also encouraged me to do a lot of work on myself. I still struggle at times with regulating my own feelings to be calm enough to help her regulate hers. And while I'm constantly working to normalize mistakes to my daughter, I'm often not as kind to myself and struggle with my own perfectionism. One thing I continue to be reminded of is that you cannot teach your child skills you don't have. You just can't. So, the work always starts from within, with your own self-awareness, growth, and learning to acknowledge your own feelings and triggers. I've never worked harder at anything in my life.

Play is a huge part of our lives, in part because of my work. We really prioritize it and make time for it, both together and independently. One thing that has really been reinforced by my motherhood journey is that children find joy and excitement in the simplest of things. It's not about reinventing the wheel, traveling a large distance, or spending a ton of money. It's about connections.

The uncertain days of my pregnancy and early motherhood magnified that there is so much we cannot control in the world. Sometimes that feels incredibly overwhelming to me. But we CAN control the kindness and love that we show to our children and others. We can work to create an environment of connection and love at home that fosters kindness. And those kind, empathetic children will take that into the world.

They will grow into kind adults. This is how the world changes. That is powerful. The work we do as mothers really does matter so much.

Motherhood has and continues to shape me in ways nothing else could - teaching me patience, unconditional love, joy on levels I didn't know I could experience, and a deeper strength I didn't know I had. Watching my daughter grow, learn, and become her own person is both humbling and amazing. And now, I'm pregnant with my second daughter and about to begin this journey, getting to know a new little person. Pregnancy already looks so different this time around for so many reasons, and I'm sure motherhood will too. I can't wait to see what this next chapter of the journey brings.

Our Steps Are Ordered

"Sometimes it happens one step, one breath, one miracle at a time!"

By Cristina P. Simmons

In 2002, we had been married for three years and were expecting our first child. I was twenty-five years old, with a background of childhood trauma and a heart that longed - more than anything to be - a "Mom." I was determined to be a perfect one. I didn't drink, and I vowed never to smoke. My own dad did when I was a child, and I always attributed my terrible allergies to secondhand smoke.

Around six months into the pregnancy, everything changed. Our hopes, dreams, and nursery plans turned into prayers, nightmares, and funeral arrangements. The doctors told us we had hit the *"gene lottery"*- the wrong kind. We carried a rare, recessive gene that caused a fatal syndrome. Our first daughter only lived for three days. The next two pregnancies ended with the same heartbreak. Three times, we experienced the 25% chance that this gene would manifest. I never saw it as a coincidence. I didn't understand it at the time, but I truly believe now that *"our steps are ordered."*

"The Lord directs our steps, so why try to understand everything along the way?"

- Proverbs 20:24 (NLT)

Before they occurred, God knew every part of our pain, and He had already begun working on our miracles. That's my prayer for you as you read this - to believe again and trust that miracles are for *you*, too. No one is excluded. My family is no more deserving than yours. I just had to believe that God's plan included me. And while I didn't trust Him perfectly (and you probably won't either), I did keep showing up with an open heart. And that's where beauty begins.

After the loss of our second daughter, I reached a breaking point. I thought I had no more tears left to cry. I began talking to my husband about adoption. We didn't know where to start, but through a series of God-orchestrated connections, we were directed to a doctor, an hour away, who had an active adoption list.

I called his office in November 2003. The nurse explained that they would be closing for the holidays and suggested that I call back after the New Year to begin the process. Although I felt oddly settled, it gave me time to convince my husband that adoption was the right step we needed to take. But the term *"settled"* was misleading. I was hurting and struggling to face the upcoming holidays. Honestly, I wanted to cancel Christmas. The thought of watching other little ones open their first gifts while I smiled through gritted teeth was unbearable. I told myself, *"Let's just skip it all this year!"* It was my plan - but not His!

Just days before Christmas, peace washed over me. I realized it wasn't anyone else's fault that I was grieving. I needed to release the resentment and celebrate others' blessings. And I did. Then came the miracle.

At 10 p.m. on Christmas Day, the phone rang. It was the doctor's office - yes, the one I'd never stepped foot in. Twin baby girls had been born and needed a home. On the night I planned to ignore Christmas entirely, God delivered the greatest gifts of my life!

We adopted those precious girls, and today they're two of the kindest, most loving young women you'll ever meet. I am forever grateful for the best living and breathing Christmas presents I've ever received.

Fast forward about four years, and the stirring returned. I felt a deep desire to be pregnant again. The outcome? He was our third child with the fatal gene - a little boy. Another loss. But, as always, God had already been working behind the scenes.

A young mother, six months pregnant with a baby boy, was looking for someone to raise her son in a way she knew she couldn't at that time in her life. That same year, I gave birth to our biological son in May, and our adopted son was born in September. Two boys: one carried in my womb, and one carried in my heart! That year, God gave us double for our trouble!

The number of small, divine details God orchestrated to make these miracles possible still amazes me! His timing! His provision! His tenderness in the waiting! All of it! I've learned that miracles aren't always big, show-stopping moments. Sometimes they come in whispers, in ordinary days. And when you look for them, you begin to see the *micro-miracles* all around you - every day!

A stranger's smile. A dragonfly that won't leave your windowsill. A flower blooming in your favorite color. An unexpected *"I love you"* from a friend. They're not coincidences. They're reminders: *God is with you.*

Planning. Healing... Some days will still feel impossible. But when you feel like you can't take one more step, promise yourself this: *"I will look for a miracle today - no matter how small!"* Healing doesn't happen *all at once.* Sometimes it happens **one step, one breath, one miracle at a time!** Our steps truly are ordered. And no matter what chapter of motherhood you're in, or how deep your pain feels - your miracle is coming, too!

Strength in the Stretch:

A Single Mother's Journey

"But God knew I needed someone not just to love me - but to love us. All of us!"

By Lacole Smith

I became a single mother at the age of twenty. That sentence still echoes in my mind some days - not with regret, but with reverence. While the world may have seen it as a setback, God was writing a story of strength.

In February 1994, I walked down the aisle full of hope, dressed in white, believing I had found forever. At that moment, I thought marriage meant stability, love, and a family that would last. But just one year later, in February 1995, my marriage had ended - and I was preparing to welcome my first child in March. Talk about a whirlwind! In twelve months, I had gone from a new wife to a single, expectant mother.

The truth is I was scared. Really scared! I was twenty, legally an adult, but still young and inexperienced when it came to life's hardest lessons. Becoming a mother was something I had looked forward to, but becoming a single mother? That was a whole different reality. But then she came. My daughter. My light. My reason.

When I held her in my arms for the first time, I knew that no matter how hard it got, I would never give up. Something shifted in me. Fear gave way to fire. Doubt gave way to devotion. My life was no longer about my plans - it was about giving her the best future I could possibly create.

Even though her father wasn't around much, his family was. They became a vital support system during those early years. His mother and father embraced our daughter like it was their own responsibility, and they loved her with a steadiness I had not expected. And while their son was absent, they chose to remain present. That kind of selfless love was a blessing I will always be grateful for.

While raising my daughter, I worked and went to school. I juggled bottles and books, late shifts and lectures, trying to stretch each hour and every dollar. There were nights when I'd be up studying with one eye open while rocking her in my arms, whispering prayers that I wouldn't fail at this job - motherhood, at womanhood, at life. It was challenging, but I kept going.

Years later, I met someone new. A man I grew close to, and eventually, we built a life together. From that relationship came three more beautiful daughters. For five years, we lived life as a family. There were joyful moments, and for a time, I thought the stability I had once dreamed of was finally mine. But life had other plans.

That relationship ended, too. And once again, I found myself alone this time raising four daughters on my own. Four little girls with big personalities, big needs, and even bigger dreams! I didn't know how I was going to do it, but I knew that I had to. There were long nights when I cried quietly in the dark, asking God for strength. There were mornings when I went to work exhausted but determined. I didn't have the luxury of giving up. My girls were watching. I knew that they needed me.

Thank God for my parents. They showed up for me in ways I could never fully describe. My mom was my constant - my rock, my sounding board, my cheerleader. She reminded me that I was doing an incredible job, even when I felt like I was failing. My dad stepped in with quiet strength, being a father figure when my girls needed one most. They helped me hold it together, one piece at a time.

And then there was my neighbor and her husband - angels in disguise. They didn't just offer help; they offered consistency. When I had to go to work or school, they watched my girls like they were their own.

When my car broke down (which happened more times than I care to count), they offered rides. When dinner seemed like a distant dream, they brought food or invited us to their table. These people - my parents, my neighbors, and a few others God placed on my path - became my village.

I moved a lot during those years. Not because I wanted to, but because I had to. Rent would go up. Jobs would change. Neighborhoods would shift. I made decisions based on what I could afford, not what I preferred. Packing up four kids and starting over more than once was exhausting, but every time we moved, I promised them - and myself - that we would move forward, not just relocate.

Now, let's talk about the car troubles! There's something humbling about sitting in a parking lot, praying your car will start so you can get your kids to school and yourself to work. But every time it cranked up, I thanked God. Because even when I didn't have everything I wanted, I had what we needed.

Then, just when I felt like I was out of strength, God sent someone into my life - my now husband. And He sent him right on time! When we started dating, I didn't know how important his presence would become. I was already in survival mode, doing everything I could to hold it all together. But God knew I needed someone not just to love me - but to love us. All of us!

Shortly after we began dating, I was in a terrible wreck. It changed everything. I was down for months - physically limited, emotionally worn out, and spiritually stretched thin. I couldn't do what I normally did. I couldn't run, drive, work, or care for my daughters the way I was used to. That's when he stepped in - not with words, but with action. He helped me so much during that time, in ways I can never repay. He showed up for my daughters like they were his own flesh and blood. He didn't see them as a burden - he saw them as a blessing. And he never hesitated to stand in the gap!

If it wasn't for him, I honestly don't know how I would've made it through that season. He helped me heal - not just physically, but emotionally. He gave me space to rest. He gave my girls security. He gave our home peace. And he did it all without expecting anything in return. It's one thing to have a man love you - but it's something altogether divine when a man loves your children with depth, consistency, and grace. He's done more for them than I can count. And because of him, they know what it feels like to be seen, safe, and loved by a father figure who chose them with his whole heart!

God has a way of putting people in position, even when we don't see it coming. My husband didn't just come into our lives - he covered us. He filled in the missing pieces. And because of him, our story changed again - not from struggle to perfection, but from survival to partnership. From exhaustion to rest. From uncertainty to stability.

I'll be honest, being a single mother of four wasn't just hard, it was spiritual. It was a daily exercise in surrender. It taught me how to stretch, how to sacrifice, how to smile when I was weary, and how to walk in faith when fear whispered in my ear. I had to trust that every ounce of effort, every sleepless night, every missed meal and every whispered prayer was planting seeds that would bloom in due time. And they did.

My daughters didn't just grow up - they flourished! They are strong, intelligent, loving, and kind. They saw their mother hustle. They saw me pray through panic, praise through pressure, and push through pain. And while I couldn't give them everything the world had to offer, I gave them something even greater: a mother who never gave up. That legacy matters to me.

My daughters are my motivation and my ministry. Every job I took, every class I passed, every tear I cried in silence - it all shaped who I became as a woman, a mother, and now, as a mentor to others walking a similar path. I didn't plan on being a single mother at twenty. But God did. He knew what He placed inside me. He knew I would rise. He knew I would turn broken pieces into building blocks. He knew that my voice would one day speak life into others who felt voiceless.

Now, when I look back, I don't just see struggle - I see strength. I see God's hand in every closed door and every new beginning. I see a girl who became a woman while raising women of her own.

To every single mother reading this: You are not alone. You are **not** a mistake. You are not failing. You are doing one of the hardest, most beautiful jobs in the world - and you are doing it well. Hold your head high. Love your children fiercely. And never forget that you are writing a legacy every single day.

The Girl I Left Behind

"That chapter of my life taught me that rock bottom doesn't mean you're done."

By Alyssa Jenice Williams

> *"I will restore to you the years that the locusts have eaten."*
> *– Joel 2:25 (NIV)*

I was fifteen when I found out I was pregnant. But my story didn't begin there - it began in the quiet ache of being raised by a single mother and feeling like I was constantly reaching for something just out of touch. My mom loved me, no doubt. She worked hard and tried to protect me in every way she knew how. But that protection often looked like isolation, and love without presence left me questioning my worth. My father wasn't around - not because she pushed him away, but because he chose not to show up. The few times he did appear were to *"discipline"* me, and even that was rare.

I was a high-achieving, honor roll student aspiring to go to Spelman and become a lawyer. I had the grades. The plan. The ambition. But underneath all that, I was a girl starving to feel loved, seen, and chosen.

That's why, when I reconnected with Thaddeus, the boy I had a crush on back in middle school, something lit up inside me. We ran into each other randomly at a bank near my house in late December 1996. Just a few minutes of small talk, but his smile? It did something to me. Not long after, I snuck out with friends to a YMCA teen dance. My mama wasn't having it, so I made the reckless choice most teenage girls make when they're desperate to taste freedom - I left and figured I'd deal with the consequences later.

That night on the dance floor changed everything. The music was loud, the lights were low, and I was finally moving like I belonged in my own skin. Then Thaddeus was behind me - his hands on my waist, his breath on my neck, his lips pressing against me like we were alone in that room. I had never felt so wanted. Not by a boy. Not by anyone.

After that, we were inseparable. He had finished school already, so I was the only one with a curfew and classes. But he would pick me up, we'd spend every moment we could together, and some nights I stayed at his house. His parents didn't mind. Mine? That was a different story. My mom did what a single mother should - she tried to keep me in line. When I didn't come home, she'd call the police to go pick me up. Not because she hated me, but because she was scared of losing me to the streets, to a boy, or to a future that didn't match all the promise she saw in me. But I didn't care. I didn't want safety. I didn't want structure. I just wanted him.

It's funny now because Thaddeus admits that first night, he was just trying to get some. Just another teenage boy chasing the moment. But something bigger happened between us. Something neither of us saw coming.

Then life took a hard left. I got arrested for shoplifting while hanging with a girl I never should've been with. It wasn't even like me. But she was doing it, and I was there. So, I did it too. And when the police asked me to call my mom, I lied. I said I lived with my uncle. But when the court date arrived… Yeah, it showed up at my real house. That didn't go well. The judge - known for being tough on teens - gave me ninety days in juvenile detention. Just like that. No warning. No probation. Just straight to jail.

I walked into that courtroom wearing Thaddeus's shirt from the night before. An honor roll student, wearing a boy's T-shirt, headed to lockup. I couldn't believe it. I couldn't believe this was my life.

When we arrived at the detention center, we had to strip, shower, and change into our new clothes. They gave me a drug test and a pregnancy test - just part of the process. I didn't think anything of it. I had just tested negative a couple of weeks before. Later that day, they pulled me into a room and sat me down.

"You're pregnant," they said.

I laughed. *"I can't be,"* I said. *"I already took a test."* But they weren't joking. Pregnant. Fifteen. In jail. I felt the floor drop from under me. A part of me was happy - this was our baby, Thaddeus's and mine. But another part of me broke wide open. I was carrying a life in a place that felt like death. I was angry at the judge, at my mom, and at my absent father. But mostly, I was angry at myself. How did I get here?

They let me call Thaddeus. He was working at a Krystal's at the time. I told him I was pregnant. That man screamed – screamed - with joy. And just like that, something in me softened. For a moment, I forgot where I was. He told me he loved me. He assured me that everything would be okay. And for a second, I believed him.

But things got harder. I started bleeding. The doctor ordered bed rest, but in jail that just meant being locked in your cell all day. I rarely left. My meals were brought to the door. The silence was suffocating. I was scared, alone, and sinking into depression. I didn't want to lose my baby. I didn't want to lose myself. Boot camp was coming soon, and the thought of going there pregnant terrified me!

Then – grace! A woman who worked with the court when I was sentenced went back to the judge on my behalf. She told him I needed rest, not punishment and care, not confinement. And he agreed. After a month and a half, I was released early. On probation - but I was home.

That chapter of my life taught me that rock bottom doesn't mean you're done. It means you're *ripe for redemption.*

To the mama reading this who feels lost in her own story, I want you to know: *Your past doesn't cancel your future. You can still rise. Still dream. Still become.* I'm no longer the girl who begged to be loved. I'm the woman who finally learned to love herself. And that girl I left behind? I went back for her, because she deserves to be whole, too!

The Mother Piece

"In healing, I learned that this wound wasn't my fault, but it was now my responsibility."

By Terry McKoy

I was fifteen the first time I became pregnant. It didn't hit me as it might for most. I didn't feel like I was becoming a mother. No soft music swelled in the background. No wave of maternal awakening washed over me. Instead, it was just the stark reality that I was having a baby. Motherhood? That was something else entirely. It didn't yet have a face, a feeling, or a form.

I grew up in a government-funded housing community, a self-proclaimed tomboy with a fire for rap lyrics and big dreams of stardom. My childhood home ran on fumes fueled by survival, shadowed by struggle. My father was behind bars. My mother held it all together the best she could, raising four children alone with grit as her only compass.

I was the youngest. And I often felt like the invisible one, caught in a whirlwind of responsibility and silence. There was no time for nurture, no room for soft landings or heart-to-hearts. So, when the doctor's visit turned into a second trimester of pregnancy, it was just another twist in a life that never slowed down.

My oldest sister had also been a teen mom, but she didn't see me as an equal in the motherhood ranks. To her, I was still the little sister who received handed-down baby clothes and cold advice, nothing more. But fate, in its strange way, offered me a lifeline.

I was enrolled in a school for pregnant teens girls like me, caught between childhood and parenthood, learning how to carry life while still figuring out how to live it. I was in 10th grade when I gave birth to my daughter. The school taught me how to diaper, budget, swaddle, and soothe. But what it couldn't prepare me for were the long, echoing silences of the night when my daughter cried and I cried too, for entirely different reasons. In those moments, I began to speak to God. Not pray. Speak.

Her early years mirrored mine. We lived in survival mode. I didn't know how to nurture, so I dressed her up and kept her clean, thinking that was enough. I was still growing up and now, she was growing up with me. After school, I worked. At night, I studied. On weekends, I craved her laughter, her wild energy, her bright eyes that scanned the world as if it were hers for the taking.

And in those weekends, a bond formed, a bond I had never known with my own mother. Something sacred. Something that felt like a whisper of healing.

By the time she was three, my son was born. And with him, I became a different mother. I had years under my belt, a little more grit - a little more know-how. But he came into a different storm, a storm of poverty, single motherhood, and generational shadows. His sister stepped up, becoming my little lieutenant, my built-in helper. He was all boy - reckless, joyful and loud. He tore through rooms like a hurricane in sneakers.

At eighteen, I packed up our life and moved into my first apartment. Alone. Determined. Tired. But alive. The years passed in a blur of permission slips, birthday candles, and growth spurts. Then came my youngest, affectionately nicknamed, *"golden child."* Born when I was twenty-one, he had what the others didn't - a home with both parents, a middle-class life, and stability.

For a while, we lived the dream. Mortgage paid. Meals cooked. Smiles captured in family portraits. But behind those photos were cracks. And by the time he was six, it shattered.

Divorce. Just like that, the illusion of *"having it all"* disappeared. And once again, I was a single mom only this time, I was raising three children with three very different beginnings. I was emotionally absent, buried in the logistics of survival. I worked. I studied. I cleaned. I fed. I provided. But I didn't feel.

He graduated with honors, went to college straight out of high school. On paper, it looked perfect. But behind his smile was silent grief. He felt like an outlier, the only child from a broken home. He carried emotional wounds I didn't see until it was too late. We both did.

And then, at forty-eight, the truth found me. Not just any truth. A truth that cracked open the foundation of my identity. I learned I was a *"Late Discovery Adoptee."* The family secret I'd unknowingly lived inside was never meant to be unearthed. But there it was - raw and undeniable.

Suddenly, the fragmented memories, the emotional distance, the aching mother wound it all made sense! The mother wound. I had passed it down unknowingly, generation to generation. An inheritance wrapped in silence and shame. I had parented with standards, structure, and sacrifice but I had neglected their emotional needs, because no one ever showed me how.

In healing, I learned that this wound wasn't my fault, but it was now my responsibility.

I look at my children, now adults, each shaped by a different version of me. They know I did the best I could with what I had, but they also know I am still learning, still growing, still becoming the mother they need me to be. Motherhood didn't find me ready, but it found me willing. And in that willingness, love was born over and over again.

The Secret Superpower

I Almost Missed

"We stood in the gap and loved her through it - just like we always do."

By Michelle Choairy

I still remember the day I found out I was pregnant with Drake. I was thirty-eight years old – experiencing a *"geriatric pregnancy"* by medical standards - and still adjusting to the fact that I had finally gotten married at thirty-six. My mom, who gifted all her daughters with a pearl necklace when they got married, had given me mine years earlier with a sigh and said, *"I don't think you're getting married, so I want you to enjoy these before it's too late."* I had received that necklace as a kind of quiet surrender - a symbol of a life she thought I might not live. But when I found out I was pregnant at thirty-eight, it felt like the story was just beginning. Motherhood has turned out to be nothing like I thought it would.

I had - and still have - a high-powered medical sales career. I was thriving professionally, managing a full territory, consistently ranked in the top twenty percent nationwide. But motherhood leveled me in the most unexpected ways.

At twenty-nine weeks, we discovered that Drake had no amniotic fluid and had stopped growing. I went from operating rooms (my medical sales job) to hospital bed rest overnight. Three weeks later, he was born via emergency C-section - just three pounds. I held him for seconds before the NICU team whisked him away. For weeks, I sat beside his ISOLETTE, not knowing what kind of future we were facing - only that we'd face it together. I learned to become a mother, not from books, but from NICU nurses - learning to handle tubes, to leave your baby in the hospital while you went home alone, and to pray he'd make it to another milestone.

What followed wasn't a straight path. Drake was fussy. Delayed. Something was off, but no one wanted to name it. I bounced from appointment to appointment, trying to convince doctors he needed help. Some questioned my credibility. Some hinted I was imagining things. The shame was crushing. But the truth? I was terrified - and profoundly alone.

Then came the turning point. At eighteen months, an occupational therapist looked me in the eye and said, *"You're not crazy. I see it too."* I cried in that office - not because of what she found, but because someone finally believed me. I don't remember her name. But I remember the feeling of being seen. Of being heard.

The years that followed were a blur of therapy appointments, specialist visits, and sleepless nights. Drake's first diagnosis was *Childhood Apraxia of Speech.* We flew across the country, leaving my newborn daughter, Rio, with family, chasing answers. And we found some. But each answer only created more questions. We navigated the complicated world of early intervention, IEPs, and insurance - all while juggling therapy appointments, learning special education laws, and trying to be the voice my son didn't yet have. All while working full-time for a major orthopedic company.

I remember the heartache of picking him up from school, unable to ask how his day was - because he couldn't answer. He didn't speak. That grief nearly swallowed me. I grieved the life I thought we'd have. The child I pictured during pregnancy. The normalcy. The ease. I grieved every time he came home and couldn't tell me what he did that day. I grieved when kids ran past him on the playground. I grieved when people said, *"He'll grow out of it,"* and I knew, deep down, he wouldn't. Somewhere inside that grief, something else was born. Not hope - at least not at first. Just a tiny seed of resolve.

I started to advocate - not just for Drake, but for myself. For my right to feel sad. For my right to be seen as both capable and exhausted. I built strength in the quiet moments sitting through IEP meetings, staying up late researching diagnoses, choosing joy when everything felt heavy.

When Drake was eight, we pursued genetic testing after years of mystery diagnoses. We discovered he had a rare condition: TBR1. At the time, he was one of only forty known kids in the world with the diagnosis. Today, that number is closer to two hundred - but his variant remains unique. One letter in his DNA flipped when he was formed. It wasn't anything I did - not the Dr. Pepper, not the Taco Bell. That diagnosis lifted years of guilt I hadn't even realized I was carrying.

Drake is now eleven. His speech still isn't always clear. He still has meltdowns. But he is the most emotionally intelligent person I've ever met. He feels deeply. He connects instantly. He talks about my late parents like he remembers them from another life.

My daughter Rio - born after a surprise pregnancy while we were preparing for IVF - is now eight. Fierce. Funny. Always cheering her brother on. She calls Drake her best friend, even when they fight like siblings do. She was hospitalized with RSV at ten days old, and I thought I would break. But we didn't. We stood in the gap and loved her through it - just like we always do. She loves him through it all. And of course, she is thriving in school and dance.

This life isn't what I expected. It's harder. It's louder. It's lonelier at times. But it's also deeper. Richer. More sacred.

Somewhere along the way, I created *Collective Wisdom for Complex Kids* and the THRIVE™ Framework - not because I had all the answers, but because I never wanted another mom to feel as alone as I once did.

Today, I still work full-time in medical sales. I still show up for IEP meetings that last hours. I still forget to drink water. I still drink too much wine. I still cry in parking lots. But I also celebrate. I advocate. I rise!

If you're reading this and feeling like you're failing - please hear me - you're not. You're becoming!

The secret superpower I almost missed wasn't in knowing all the therapies. It was in learning to let go of the dream and embrace the child I had. In choosing love over fear. In seeing progress not in milestone - but in moments. Drake's superpower is love. Mine is resilience. And yours? Maybe it's rising again. Or showing up when you're bone-tired. Or holding grief and joy in the same breath.

Whatever it is - don't miss it. It just might be the very thing that carries you - and your child - home.

The Unsacred Silence

"That night, I finally told the truth. Not to anyone else - just to myself."

By Jackie Nole

I remember the night I decided I wouldn't stay quiet anymore. It wasn't loud. It wasn't violent. It didn't look like a dramatic movie scene. It looked like me, sitting in my car, pregnant, and telling myself, *"Enough is enough."* That night, I finally told the truth. Not to anyone else - just to myself.

I admitted that the life I thought I had built around faith and family was simply a depiction of my imagination because it was tainted with lies and abandonment. It was dead. I had endured betrayal, manipulation, and judgment in the name of righteousness. I had tried to pray the pain away. Scream it away. Smile it away. And all it had done was erased little by little.

But that night, I heard my voice for the first time in years. And she whispered, *"This isn't what God meant when He said, 'love.'"*

The Illusion

For years, I wore my marriage like a badge of honor. More than anyone, my maternal family saw it firsthand. We were the picture of faith-filled commitment. I was the devoted wife - modest, loyal, and deeply in love. He was the husband I believed God had called me to serve beside. People admired how young we were and how *"grounded"* we seemed to be despite our age. They said we were *"doing it right,"* and how proud of us they were.

But behind closed doors, I had a husband who had ideologies that had nothing to do with love. I was taught that a good woman forgives, forgets, and submits. That questioning was rebellion, and silence was strength. A wife also covers her husband's sins with grace and keeps the family looking whole, no matter the cost. So, when the cheating started, I told no one.

I was already a mother. I had a baby on the way and a sweet, three-year-old girl watching me. I was also a woman of faith, and I believed walking away would hurt my children and my faith. And more than anything, I feared being a bad mother. Scared that if I left, I would be labeled as the traitor and the problem. So, I stayed. I prayed. And I started to slowly disappear. I stopped laughing the way I used to. I stopped dreaming. My world shrank to the size of keeping peace - inside my home, inside the church, inside my own body.

I began to believe that suffering was the same as being righteous, and silence was sacred. But truth has a way of breaking through, even in whisper in my case, in vociferous fits. One day, after another apology that didn't change. Another caught lie, I couldn't help but become the most bitter version I had ever felt. The ugly kind. Darkness and feelings of anger so deep that it felt like it swallowed me whole. That day, it was different. I felt the betrayal not only towards me but towards my children. It haunted me.

I knew that behind my faith and loyalty was a girl whose mother had gone through a horrendous marriage of abuse and betrayal. So, growing up, I had been silenced. I was a girl who had been taught not to question. Not to speak. Not to ask for more. And that girl? She was still in there. Tired. Heartbroken. But still in there.

Memories flooded my head of my abused mother and all I could think was: *"What kind of love do I want my children to see?"* Not the kind that makes you disappear. Not the kind that makes you beg for basic respect with futile results. I realized then that the silence I had protected for so long was killing me. And that breaking it wasn't betrayal - it was deliverance. But God only knows the struggle I was experiencing through every cell in my body - resisting to break the silence.

The Leap

Leaving wasn't graceful. It wasn't like the stories where people cheer for your bravery and surround you with warmth. It was lonely, ugly and extremely complicated. People said I was abandoning my family and that cheating wasn't something we speak about. We just accepted it and kept going.

"Do it for the good of the family. Men will be men - it's normal."

A good wife stays and makes it work. Leaving meant that I would be acting out of pride and an unforgiving heart. Surely, not the thing God honors. I was told that I should have prayed harder, tried more, and forgiven again. But I kept moving. Not because I was sure of the outcome - but because staying had become too painful to bear. But even bigger than that was the image of the crushed look on my children's faces when their father kept making excuses for being a liar and a traitor. So, I couldn't stay long enough to see and endure that.

When I separated and was finally divorced, many family members criticized me. Friends whispered. Even my children questioned me for a time. And honestly? I questioned myself. The judgment was sharp. But do you know what cut even deeper? The realization that I had been teaching my children, especially my daughter, that love looks like enduring disrespect. That forgiveness means tolerating repeated harm. That spirituality means staying silent. I couldn't do that anymore. Not for them. Not for me. So, I stepped away from the marriage, from the shame, and from the version of faith that required me to suffer in silence.

The Becoming

In the aftermath of divorce and the echoes of harmful childhood ideologies, I embarked on a journey of healing. Therapy became a space where I unlearned the gaslit beliefs that were too much to handle, too dramatic, or somehow unworthy of love. I challenged the patterns of pain passed down through generations of women in my family - my grandmother and mother, who deserved so much more than they were given.

Their struggles fueled my determination to say, *"Enough is enough. I deserve better."* Somewhere along the way, I began to hear myself again. I began to trust my gut. I began to speak truth without shaking. Healing wasn't quick. It came in waves - therapy, reflection, raw honesty, and grace. I stumbled into new mistakes. I found myself in other unhealthy relationships.

Through years of introspection and hard work, I learned to love myself the way my grandmother and mother should have loved themselves - with the recognition that their beauty, strength, and worth were never defined by their circumstances. I chose to see myself through the lens of their hopes and dreams, understanding that my journey could be a redemptive testament to their sacrifices.

This healing journey wasn't about erasing the past but about transforming it into a foundation of strength. It was about reclaiming my worth, choosing a partner who aligned with my values, and understanding that my story could inspire others. It was about breaking cycles, standing tall, and knowing that I deserve a life filled with love and respect.

In loving myself as others deserved to be loved, I found the strength to become the woman I was always meant to be, and in doing so, I honor the legacy of the women who came before me. Their dreams live on in me, and through my journey. I hope to light the way for others.

Today, I'm accomplishing more than I ever thought possible. I am a mother again to a beautiful baby boy, owner of a children's clothing line, a podcaster and an author. And I'm not finished! My story hasn't ended.

My Message to You

If you are reading this, and you've ever swallowed your truth to make someone else comfortable - this is for you. If you've ever mistaken suffering for righteousness, I see you. If you've ever thought, *"Maybe I'm just too much, too sensitive, too dramatic."* I promise you're not. You are just waking up and starting to voice what your soul is crying out. I wrote this chapter not because I've arrived, but because I've survived. And survival has given me a voice I refuse to silence ever again.

I don't know where you are in your story. But I hope mine reminds you that silence is not sacred. Truth is. And your voice is holy ground. Don't silence it ever again.

The Day My Legacy Began

*"There were no cries, no chaos. Just the quiet weight of eternity
brushing against my cheek."*

By Debbie Simmons

Some call it *"April Fool's Day."* I call it the day everything changed. It was the day I became a mother. And the day I let go. In a hospital room filled with hopes and heartbreak, I held each of my sons - *Zach, Josh, Nate,* and *Chris* - as they entered and exited this world in the same breath. My heart, once overflowing with dreams of lullabies, soccer games, and scraped knees, was cracked wide open by the unimaginable. Yet, in that unbearable grief, something sacred took root. A legacy.

Infertility had already tested every ounce of my faith and strength. After years of waiting, praying, and enduring the heartbreak of *"not yet,"* we were gifted a miracle pregnancy through a fertility study - then shocked to discover it was not one, not two, but four babies. The excitement was palpable. The fear was all-consuming. And the love? It was deeper than I had ever known.

At twenty-six weeks, I went into early labor. The details blur now - the frantic rush to the hospital, the hum of machines, the kind yet helpless expressions from nurses. One by one, my boys came. One by one, they left. Zach wrapped his hand around my finger as if to say, *"I see you, Mama."* Josh, Nate, and Chris followed. There were no cries, no chaos. Just the quiet weight of eternity brushing against my cheek.

People often ask, *"How did you survive that?"* The answer is simple, "I didn't. Not the woman I was." The version of me that walked into that hospital room full of anticipation and nursery plans didn't walk out. A different woman emerged. One marked by sorrow, yes. But also, by surrender.

Because on that day - in that moment of ultimate devastation - I placed a stake in the ground. *"God,"* I prayed through tears, *"I have no idea how to move forward. But I will trust You."* There were no promises.

No blueprints. Only the invitation to take one breath. Then one step. Then another.

The questions that haunted me were *"Why? Why us? Why them? Why this way?"* But over time, I realized that even if God answered my *"whys,"* it wouldn't bring my boys back. And in eternity, the *"whys"* won't matter. Because heaven holds no sorrow, and my boys are there. Whole. Joyful. Waiting.

Instead, I began asking, *"How do I survive this?"* God's whisper came gently, *"Take the next best step."*

So, I did. I learned to mark progress not in miles, but in inches. Some days, victory looked like brushing my teeth. Other days, it was making it through a church service without tears. And always, it was clinging to the truth that God was still good - even when life was not.

That question led to healing. And eventually, it led to a new question: *"How do I thrive?"*

That shift, from surviving to thriving, birthed an unplanned but beautiful journey of adoption, ministry, and motherhood reimagined. Over time, our family grew to include nine adopted children. Each child brought their own story, their own scars, and their own piece of my healing. My arms, once empty, became full. My home, once silent, now overflowed with laughter, challenges, and sacred chaos.

We didn't become a picture-perfect family. We became something better - a picture of redemption. Of God restoring the years the locusts had eaten. Of beauty rising from ashes.

God continued to plant seeds in my heart to do more. He led me to found *Anchor Point,* a ministry that stands for life, healing, and legacy with my friend, Melissa Conway. There, we walk with women facing unplanned pregnancies, equip families with resources to thrive, and provide safe, faith-filled places for restoration. I am blessed to be *"Lolli"* to a tribe of grandbabies. I often sit with grieving mothers, counsel weary parents, and teach others how to walk through loss with a faith that doesn't falter.

Each of those moments is a thread in the tapestry of legacy. And none of that would have happened without April 1st. Zach, Josh, Nate, and Chris never spoke a word. But their lives speak through mine. Their impact echoes in the halls of *Anchor Point*, in every family we serve, in every woman I hug and whisper to, *"You are not alone."*

Because of them, I love more fiercely. I grieve with others more deeply. I believe more fully that God can take the broken pieces of our stories and craft something eternal. Even now, decades later, April 1st is never just another day. It's a day I remember how far God has brought me. I remember. I weep. I worship. I celebrate. And I smile at the thought that in heaven, four boys are cheering me on.

Even on the hardest day, love never left. It became a legacy. And that legacy lives on - every April 1st, and every day in between.

So, to the mother with empty arms, the woman with shattered dreams, the one who wonders if joy is still possible - I see you. I was you. And I can promise: *Legacy can rise from loss. Not in spite of it. But through it!*

Me.3

"Another baby, a new chance to 'do it right,'
But the glow faded into silence at night."

By Lauren Stewart

I wanted to be the first to drive,
The first to travel, to feel alive.
But fate had written a different scene,
A baby in arms at just eighteen.
While my friends walked the expected track,
Uni halls, wild nights, no looking back.
I was learning lullabies trying to do things right,
battling sleepless delirium night after night.
I'd worked with kids, I thought I knew,
But nothing prepares you for something so new.
Grateful, yes, but heavy too!
Lonely days with a love so true.
They called it *postnatal depression*,
But it felt like a quiet, aching confession.
No pride, no joy, just playing the part,
Each nappy change chipped away at my heart.
I worked hard, smiled wide, kept it together,
While storms raged inside through every weather.
ADHD (still undiagnosed)
People-pleasing deeply enclosed.
But I did it…I raised a son full of grace,
My boy, my mirror, my saving place.
His father involved, though we lived apart,
And somehow, I built a home with heart.
Then came a man who felt like "the one,"
A family man who felt warm like the sun.
I moved to a village, became part of a clan,
Craving the closeness I never quite had.
Another baby, a new chance to "do it right,"
But the glow faded into silence at night.
We became strangers in familiar space,
And I packed up my hope, left with grace.
Singledom again, and peace for a while,
Then dating apps promised a spark, a smile.

A charmer arrived, swept me off my feet,
Love-bombed and vanished in bitter retreat.
Next came a man who became my spouse,
A child on the way, a new family, a house.
On social media we looked like the dream,
But inside, we unravelled seam by seam.
I craved connection, he sought his own way,
And slowly my light started fading each day.
Years of confusion, shame and strain,
Until one day it ended in heartbreak and pain.
That's when I turned inward and began to see,
The wounds from childhood still living in me.
A little girl who'd never felt enough,
Who learned to settle for love that was rough.
Through therapy's light and learning my style,
I saw how I'd chased approval for miles.
Attachment wounds and people-pleasing,
Kept me in places far from healing.
But healing came, slow… but sure,
Layer by layer, I searched for the *pure*.
Like peeling an onion, the sting ran deep,
Each truth uncovered woke wounds from sleep.
Tears fell as I faced the past,
But with every peel, I found peace at last.
I learned my worth, reclaimed my voice,
And saw, at last, I'd made the right choice.
Not cursed. Not broken. Just never shown,
That my value was mine, and mine alone.
I studied, I trained, I rose once more,
Turned my pain into purpose, to something *more*.
Now I guide others through the storm,
As a Somatic Coach, where healing is born.
Specialised in abuse recovery,
I help people come back to *who they were always meant to be*.

To see they're worthy, whole, complete,
To rise again on steady feet.
No shame now for "three kids, three dads,"
No space left for guilt or judgment's fads.
I've worked hard, and I've come so far…
My children, my heart, my guiding stars!

So here I stand, unmasked and free
A mother, a woman...
Finally me!

Shattered into Wholeness

"I had to believe I was worthy of love - freely given, not earned."

By Robyn Whitworth

I prayed that my life would have a lasting legacy, but I felt that opportunity was cut short due to complications of my last pregnancy.

"Where is my baby? How is the baby? Is she alright? Have you seen her? Who is with her?" My mom's soft voice came through the fog of post anesthesia, *"Yes, she is beautiful, four pounds, nine ounces. She's doing well in the NICU with her daddy."*

I was barely thirty-four weeks pregnant when I went into surgery earlier that day, not knowing if I'd live to see another day. I'll never know all the details of that birth. My body trembled from trauma and medication as I tried to find my bearings in the ICU. My mom stayed with me that day - then my sister. Then Mom came back again, trading shifts with my husband over four long days. On the fourth day, after a blood transfusion, I finally had enough energy to get to the bathroom alone and change my tiny baby's diaper in the NICU down the hall.

That's when the nurse walked in. Her words stopped me. "Your insurance won't cover more days here. You've been out of ICU for two days. Your chart says you're stable. You have four hours to prepare for discharge." I froze. My mom looked at me with alarm. My husband looked like he wanted to fight someone. I did not feel well enough to go home. I could barely stand! Did they know I didn't even live in this city? Home was four hours away in another state. I felt numb.

My husband advocated for help. The social worker found a room at a nearby charity house seven minutes away, so I could stay close to our baby and recover a bit more. The angel that my mother had been from the very first day of my pregnancy helped me get dressed, gathered my medications, wheeled me downstairs, and then she went to get the car.

I sat in the hospital entrance, barely alive. People moved past me, walking and talking with ease. I stared out of the glass doors at the falling snow and thought, *"Is this really what's supposed to happen after major, life-threatening abdominal surgery? Five days ago, I was told to say my goodbyes... and now I'm being told to move on?"* My baby was somewhere in that massive building - and I was being sent away.

The numbness cracked the second the car door closed. I broke down as the hot, heavy tears began to fall without end. I couldn't speak. My mom was there, but she didn't ask me to. She seemed to know my thoughts. She knew the weight of my sorrow, confusion, and pain. She knew the tears that fell were necessary.

When we arrived at the charity house, she checked me in, wheeled me to a small room, removed my coat, helped me into bed, and promised to wake me for my meds. That night, I had a dream. I was in a dark room, standing on a slick, black floor. Suspended in the air was a glowing red heart - my heart! Suddenly, it shattered into tiny pieces, falling in every direction. My gut sank. My soul screamed. Then someone walked in and picked up a piece.

It was Jesus! He smiled gently and pressed the piece into the light, beginning to reassemble my broken heart. My mom came in and picked up a piece. Then my husband, then a friend, a neighbor, my sister... until hundreds of people were there, smiling, helping, holding their hands and mine. For the first time in my life, I felt beautiful and unequivocally supported. I asked, *"Why so much pain? To bring support? Is this really possible for me?"*

I heard Jesus speak. *"Our hearts break to make room for more others... to allow our light to shine brighter. Look!"*

I looked up and saw my heart - bigger than before! The breaks had become avenues of light!

"Will it break again?" I asked.

"Yes. And we will help you put it back together every time. Your heart will grow, and your light will shine brighter. I will be here, holding you together as often as you ask. Please teach the Mothers," He said.

"The world will change, when we can change the modeling to the Mothers. Let your light shine, my beautiful daughter. Teach the Mothers."

I woke with sudden hope, deep gratitude. I had found a *holy* understanding. Two and a half weeks later, I went home with my five-pound miracle! We healed together over the next year. Since then, I've applied the lesson God taught me. It wasn't easy. I had to prune old beliefs from misunderstood religious teachings and generational fear-based modeling.

My first four children had a mom who parented mostly in fear - fear of doing it wrong, fear of not being enough, fear of failing them. I tried to control everything - schedules, behavior, and even outcomes. But after that NICU experience, I understood something sacred: *"I never had to control. I had to love."* Even more so was the deep-seated belief that change was always possible!

I had to allow support, and I had to receive it. I had to believe I was worthy of love - freely given, not earned. I had to release the need to prove my value. I had to risk looking imperfect and trust that I am still in the arms of God! That truth changed everything!

Now, I reach BIG goals alongside motherhood - without guilt. I feel confident in every choice, knowing that I am fully held in Jesus, regardless of the outcome. If I act from love, there's nothing to fear! I wrote down the process I went through to transform my mind and renew my soul. Then I created a space for women to do the same, if they feel called.

The ripple effect of my willingness to choose belonging, to choose reformation, to choose absolute LOVE in every interaction has proved God's mighty hand in answering my desire to leave a lasting legacy on this planet. I've been able to touch hundreds of mothers' lives, who are now teaching their children and their grandchildren.

To the mom who is reading this, you are not alone, unless you choose to be. The world believes in disconnection and loneliness. You aren't the world. You are a divine being! You are part of the story of Mothers - a story of support, a story where LOVE is the force that heals, sustains, and transforms. You always hold the pen to your life story.

Drop judgment! Drop perfection! Drop fear! Drop competition and comparison! I have re-parented myself with these beliefs, and the far-reaching effect has been beautiful to witness! My children know unconditional love. My children have a mother who is confident, reaches her dreams, has no guilt and doesn't sacrifice herself in vainly pursuing some level of worthiness to take up space.

Choose to write your story with support and love - and watch how your hope and possibilities multiply!

"Be not conformed to this world: but be ye transformed by the renewing of your mind, that ye may prove what is that good, and acceptable, and perfect will of God."

- Romans 12:2

Empowerment Through Challenges:

Navigating the Stages of Motherhood

"As I walked across the stage, one of my boys screamed, 'That's my Mom!'"

By Danielle Booher

In March 2003, I was seven months pregnant while my two-year-old son and I were living in a homeless shelter. Even though my parenting journey started when I was eighteen, I never could have imagined that I would have ended up homeless. Tae *(my second son)* was born with eczema, colic, and acid reflux which meant he would have trouble sleeping through the night. I had postpartum depression and was just trying to survive. We only lived in the shelter until Tae was a few months old.

I made a few mistakes and ended up getting back with Tae's father who was very abusive, both physically and mentally. We started living together again and I got pregnant. I was working at Denny's and got promoted to manager. One night I arrived at work and ten minutes into my shift, I knew that something was wrong. I sat down at the bar across from the kitchen and five minutes later, my water broke! I was only twenty-five weeks pregnant. I was in denial, and I didn't want to go to the hospital, but I had no other choice. I delivered my son in the ambulance, but he was stillborn. I was devastated but still in denial. When I arrived at the hospital, the EMT placed my son on the counter in the hospital room, wrapped up in what looked like a newspaper instead of my arms.

I was bleeding so I was unable to get up and hold him. Finally, I asked *"Can I hold my son?"* Sadly, I didn't know that I could advocate for my son or myself, so I suffered in silence. As I was hemorrhaging, I was told that I had three choices: I could get Pitocin and give birth to the placenta, get the D & C surgery, or I could die! I told them I didn't want to choose because I had already lost my son, and I didn't want to give birth to the placenta. The response was, *"Do you want to die?"* I didn't, so I received Pitocin and gave birth to the placenta. I had to receive two units of blood to save my life as well.

Afterwards, I ended up leaving Dennys and my abusive Ex. I became a manager for another restaurant and decided that I would move closer to my extended family. So, the boys and I moved to Ohio, and I was transferred to a restaurant there. My second son was diagnosed with ADHD, Aspergers and bipolar disorder. I knew I had to do something different, and I have always wanted to help people, so I decided that I would start my prerequisites and try to become a Nurse. I was juggling working two jobs, school, Tae's multiple appointments each week and life in general.

On July 25, 2010, I received the phone call that changed my life forever. *"Hello,"* the voice said. *"Matthew has a gun."*

I was in shock and denial! I listened to my Mom and my brother go back and forth when finally, I heard *"Do you hear your sister?"* I said, *"We love you and your daughter needs you."* And then, I heard a gunshot!

I went from the most extroverted person to shut down and become what I call a *"zombie robot"* and I was on autopilot! I wanted to quit nursing school before I started, but ultimately, I knew I had to give my children a better life, which is my *"WHY?"*

I started a relationship and by October 2010, my new boyfriend and his four-year- old son, and my two sons were living together. Becoming a bonus Mom to that precious four-year-old saved me in many ways. While in Nursing school, I started planning my wedding with the help of my amazing sister! Life was challenging, and I was working three days a week and attending nursing school six days a week. I tried to quit nursing school three times, but thank goodness, I didn't, and I ended up graduating. As I walked across the stage, one of my boys screamed, *"That's my Mom!"*

All of the emotions flooded my body, and I was so grateful and proud that I didn't give up!

A few weeks later, we got married and a few more weeks later, we found out we were pregnant with my daughter. The marriage did not go so great, and I eventually left the state of Ohio and moved to Georgia with three kids, some clothes and some important documents. Unfortunately, I couldn't bring my youngest son, because I did not adopt him, which was devastating! However, as a single mother with three kids, I had to keep pushing. I got my Nursing license in Georgia and found a job. We were blessed to be able to stay with my Mom for a few months until we had a place of our own.

2022 was the year I was turning 40 and my whole life changed at that moment. My boyfriend at the time encouraged me to try things I always wanted to try. So, I became a stand-up comedian which gave me the courage to start my own podcast. By August 2022, I went on a forgiveness journey and became a life coach. At that moment, I realized that I was not healed from many traumatic events in my life - especially my brother's passing. I felt so guilty for not being able to save his life, but in that moment, I realized there was nothing I could have done to save him, and the weight was lifted off my shoulders. I finally forgave myself and others, and I was free.

In many ways, my life started over at that point, and I found my purpose. I found forgiveness in my heart and eliminated limiting beliefs to help me move forward and heal - and so can you! The first step to eliminating limiting beliefs is to journal or make a list of what others, and yourself have been telling you. Practicing small wins also helped me eliminate limiting beliefs. I would start small goals for myself and then when

I achieved the goal, I would celebrate having done so. I also say positive affirmations every day, which has been extremely helpful. When it comes to forgiveness remember that it is for you - not them - and doing so, helps you get back control.

As you can see, I have played many roles in my motherhood journey, and I have learned from every one of them. I have learned that no parent is perfect and to not dwell on the mistakes that I made in the past. After all, we cannot go back into the past and change our mistakes. We can only grow and learn from them and change our actions in the future. It's important to show yourself grace and always aim for your best. That's all we can do. On the toughest days, remember your *"Why?"* (reason/motivation) and keep going.

Always remember that you are not alone. Don't ever be afraid to ask for help because there may be resources available. Most importantly, believe in yourself and never give up!

Warrior Mother:

Remembering Divine Strength

"...beneath these challenges lies an opportunity to remember who we truly are... divine beings raising divine beings."

By Sonya Achara

The Marine Corps taught me to push beyond physical limits, to stand tall under pressure, and to lead with unwavering resolve. For fourteen years, I embodied the warrior spirit, breaking barriers as a woman in a male-dominated world. I became a black belt martial arts instructor, competed in bodybuilding competitions, and led Marines with the kind of strength that commanded respect.

But nothing - not boot camp, not combat training, not even deployment to Afghanistan - prepared me for the battle that would truly reveal my power: motherhood in the shadow of narcissistic abuse.

The Perfect Illusion

When I met my son's father, he showed me what I thought was love in its purest form. He was attentive, affectionate, and seemingly devoted. *"He gets me,"* I thought, mistaking love bombing for genuine connection. The red flags were there - subtle at first, then impossible to ignore. But by then, I was pregnant with our son.

The birth of my beautiful boy should have been the beginning of our family story. Instead, it marked the acceleration of a nightmare. The man who once couldn't keep his hands off me now avoided physical contact. The person who promised to build an empire with me began sabotaging our financial foundation. The father who took endless photos with our infant son was performing for an audience that didn't include me.

"Your mom never loved you. Your tranny daddy never loved you. I never loved you," he spat during one particularly vicious argument when our son was six months old. The words cut deep, designed to reopen childhood wounds of emotional neglect. In that moment, I saw clearly what I

had denied for too long: this wasn't love. This was *warfare against my spirit.*

The Impossible Choice

By the time our son turned one, I faced the choice that would define my motherhood: stay in material comfort while my soul withered or leave with nothing but my child and my dignity.

I chose my son's spirit over everything else. The day I left, I knew it wouldn't be simple. What I couldn't have anticipated was how he would systematically work to destroy what we had built. He kicked tenants out of our rental properties to force foreclosure. He manipulated evidence to paint me as unstable. He fought for joint legal custody - not because he wanted to parent, but because he wanted leverage.

"If he falls down the stairs, it's your fault," he shouted one day as I tried to leave our son with him, running down the stairs while dangerously carrying our toddler. In that moment, I realized this wasn't just about me anymore. My son's emotional and physical safety hung in the balance.

The Spiritual Battlefield

The courtroom became my new battlefield - one where physical strength meant *nothing,* and spiritual fortitude meant *everything.* I discovered that maintaining high vibration in the face of triggering accusations was more powerful than any legal strategy. I documented everything without emotion. I set firm boundaries without anger. I focused on patterns rather than diagnoses. Most importantly, I refused to be energetically triggered during proceedings.

"Your Honor," I said, during one particularly tense hearing, *"I'm not here to vilify my son's father. I'm here to ensure our son has the stability and safety he deserves."* The judge's eyes met mine, and in that moment of authentic truth, something shifted in the courtroom energy.

Despite his elaborate attempts to paint me as unstable, I was awarded full legal and physical custody. Despite his financial sabotage, our properties remained protected until I secured a court-ordered sale. This wasn't luck - it was the power of maintaining spiritual sovereignty in chaos.

The Quantum Healing

Before I had my son, the anxiety the Marine Corps used to give me had taken its toll. I found myself drinking bottles of wine just to numb the anxiety. The struggles of raising a boy while going through a messy divorce also didn't help. My hands developed a constant tingling sensation that doctors attributed to alcohol damage. I was functioning but not thriving - surviving but not living.

Then, six months ago, something extraordinary happened. While listening to a Joe Dispenza meditation about women reclaiming their power, I felt compelled to write the mantras, breathwork and meditations down and started doing them three times a day. I experienced what I can only describe as quantum healing. In an instant - not gradually, not with practice, but in a single moment of divine connection - my anxiety disappeared. My alcohol cravings vanished. The tingling in my hands subsided.

I had stepped into a different reality - one where I remembered who I truly was beneath the trauma, beneath the military training, and beneath the motherhood struggles. I was divine energy having a human experience, not a human struggling to find energy.

Conscious Motherhood

This awakening transformed my approach to motherhood. I realized that my son chose me as his mother for this exact journey. He knew what he was getting - a warrior who would protect his spirit at all costs, a woman who would remember her divine nature even in the darkest moments!

Now, our mornings begin with gratitude practices. We spend time in nature, grounding our energy in the earth. When big emotions arise - as they do for any toddler - I help him name them rather than shame them. *"It's okay to feel angry,"* I tell him. *"Let's breathe through it together."*

When his father attempts to manipulate our communication or uses our son as a pawn, I maintain boundaries without resentment. *"We follow the court order,"* I explain calmly, both to my Ex and to my son when he's old enough to understand. *"This keeps everyone safe and respected."*

The greatest gift I can give my son isn't protection from all pain - it's showing him how to process pain with dignity. It isn't shielding him from all challenges - it's demonstrating how to face challenges with spiritual strength.

The Ripple Effect

My journey from Marine to mother, from victim to victor, has become more than my personal healing path. It has become my purpose. Through my podcast *"Remember Who You Are 222,"* I now guide conscious professionals through their spiritual awakening and truth seeking in a world filled with social conditioning. As a published author of *"Remember Who You Are: My Journey to Higher Consciousness"* and speaker on conscious leadership, I bridge the gap between spiritual wisdom and practical application.

I teach them quantum embodiment techniques that create breakthrough results in business and life. I show them how to maintain elevated consciousness during challenging situations without becoming emotionally reactive. Most importantly, I help them remember their divine nature when everything external tries to make them forget, enabling them to lead from authentic power rather than conditioned patterns.

My work demonstrates that spiritual awakening isn't separate from professional success. It's the foundation for creating impact that transcends conventional limitations.

Motherhood isn't perfect - it's *perfectly imperfect.* The sleepless nights, the court battles, the moments of doubt are all part of the journey. But beneath these challenges lies an opportunity to remember who we truly are... *divine beings raising divine beings.*

My son watches me now with curious eyes as I meditate each morning. Sometimes he crawls into my lap, placing his small hands on mine. In these quiet moments, I realize that the greatest lesson of motherhood isn't what we teach our children with words, but what we show them through our resilience.

I am not just raising my son - I am raising the man who will one day impact this world. By healing my wounds, by standing in my power, by remembering my divine nature, I create ripples that will extend far beyond my lifetime.

This is the legacy of the warrior mother: not perfect but perfectly committed to growth. Not unscathed, but beautifully scarred with wisdom. Not defined by battles lost, but by the divine strength remembered in the midst of the fight!

The Mother to Many

"However large the number grows and however I got them, they are all mine."

By Sumika Gilford

Every mother's journey is different. It's a mom's job to not only care for a child and help clear their path to navigate in society but also to learn them and cultivate the things that make them special. There's no pay, no orientation telling you how things should go or what to do if there's a problem, no specified training, no reset button, and no customer service chat bubble. There's only one-of-a-kind experience with a one-of-a-kind child. It's not a job you can learn from a book or the Internet, you have to trust your heart and your decisions and jump in with both feet. I've jumped many times. Biological children, an open adoption, stepchildren, godchildren, grandchildren, and even "accepted" children that came into my life and never left. They're all very different and all come from very different circumstances, but they are all mine.

I had my first child at 20, unmarried in the military, involved with a man who had a secret relationship I knew nothing about for a year until a couple of months before I delivered. I left the relationship but decided my child was my priority. That child that I carried ended up being the foundation for everything I would come to know about love and everything I didn't know that God had planned for me. I learned patience, overprotection, all the songs in Blues Clues, and how to think on my feet. How to run a business on 2 hours of sleep that were determined by his schedule, how to budget, how to plan, and how much someone learns from you just by watching. That playtime is sometimes no words just sound effects, behind doors are always the best hiding spots, and that I was a part of someone's bigger picture.

My son was smart, amazing and I was in awe. He was so high-energy and had the most infectious smile that made me feel like this could be my little world forever.

Unexpectedly, in a new relationship, my daughter came three years later. A tiny little bundle of gorgeous that made me feel like I knew nothing. She didn't like Blue's Clues, she would rather play by herself than play hide and seek and she wasn't all dolls and bows like TV made me think she would be. She was books, music, and nonstop words. I didn't understand why everything I thought I knew didn't work. She watched me, mimicked me, and taught me that I can't just say what to do, I have to show how to be. She wanted to dress like me, talk like me, and even date people with the same qualities as the people I dated when she got older because she was learning to love like me. It was jaw-dropping to see how much influence my choices as a mom could have. The two of them taught me that the 19-year-old me who had no children was selfish but the Mommy me had a huge capacity to love and to change not just for me but for them.

That love was tested with the following child. An abusive relationship and that same capacity to love forced me to make the hardest decision I would ever have to make. I put my third child up for adoption to give him a better life than I could safely offer at the time. I vetted couples for months, changed my mind a few times, and finally settled on an open adoption where they and I would keep in contact so I could see him grow in a good environment. His adoptive mother is amazing, and I love her for stepping in to offer the peaceful and loving life I wish I could have given.

Due to life-threatening health issues, at 24, I lost the ability to have any more kids. It was painful to think I could never have a child with my husband, but God decided I wasn't done yet. In came the godchildren, the son from my first marriage, more godchildren, the "adult kids" who were much younger but still needed love and nurturing that I was available to give, the grand girls, the kids that just grew to call me "ma" and stayed in my kitchen, and my youngest son from my current marriage. However large the number grows and however I got them, they are all mine. They pop up on holidays and offer random hugs. They call when they need to talk or just want to tell me what they saw me on social media that day. They request cashapps and demand to hear that they are the favorite. They replenish me. They feed my ambitions and say affirming words. They make me laugh. They make my heart hurt for them. They make me afraid for them. They make me proud and make me want the world for them. They make me want to be great for them.

That's what being a mom is: the synergy of giving small humans everything they need, and they give you everything your heart wants. You see them grow and evolve and become these people with imaginative ambitions and realistic goals. You watch them climb and stumble all while trying not to let them see that you're holding your hands out to catch them because "Mom, I got this." You get unhinged when they make choices you know may not be the best but still console them in the aftermath. You brag on the smallest accomplishments because it feels like "we" did it. Being a mother has been my hardest test and my greatest joy and I'm grateful for it all.

I Love My Kids, But!

"I love my kid, but I still love my career…
Luckily, God had another plan for me, yet again."

By Tiffany Ludwicki

I am not sure how you feel, but I often get a chuckle by the title of this chapter; followed almost immediately by a sigh of relief, as the person hearing it feels supported by their own internal struggles around parenthood. This is likely due to the fact that before becoming a parent, we had freedom to quickly come and go as we pleased. We could shower, clean the house, read a book, and even use the restroom without constant interruptions. Now, routine ventures seem almost impossible at times, because of the demands of today's world. Today families are forced to have dual earning households, making it very challenging to create a work-life balance, especially in a patient, playful atmosphere that fosters security and exploration. I found it hard anyway.

While at work, I longed to be with my kids, even though I loved my job. When I was at home, I wished I was at work because I struggled to play their games. Using my imagination was hard, unlike the confidence I had at work. I love my kids... but I also missed the uninterrupted flow of state and cleanliness of the pre-kids era.

You see, I never planned on having kids, however I must interject that I love them dearly, and am so grateful they changed the course of my life! A year after I invested in my independent dental hygiene practice, I found out I was three and half months pregnant. Six months later, as I was about to give birth, Covid shut down the world! I had to shut down my clinic, literally dismantling shelves and taking them off the walls, moving equipment using my car and filling every empty space in my garage, while sparing my bedroom and closets. I was left wondering where I could reopen my business, when should I return to work to save what I built so far, and how I could manage childcare and work around nursing a baby. I was forced, like most people, to reevaluate what truly mattered in life and learn how to build resilience.

I have to admit, I enjoyed the isolation of this time because I was tired, of course – you're a mom, so I'm sure you can understand. In my case, my baby was having difficulty sleeping, she was snoring and actually having moments of sleep apnea. Although I was contemplating how to get back to work, and how I could find quality sleep throughout the day, I knew I had to do something for my baby. Sleep apnea and breathing issues were red flags for proper physical and emotional growth in children. She didn't have enlarged tonsils or adenoids. She wasn't the typical forty-year-old obese man to be given a CPAP so she wouldn't even be prescribed a CPAP at her age, despite the diagnosis, nor would I want that to be her future. All I knew at this point was that I was going to find out how I could help my baby. I love my kids, but... the rabbit hole that brought me down - WOW!

I enrolled in a program for my functional therapy (something that could help reduce sleep apnea events) which only dental hygienists and SLPs could train to practice. How divinely orchestrated that I was a Dental Hygienist! During this training, I actually resolved my snoring, improved my memory and increased my energy. This is where I really learned how bad snoring was for mental and physical health.

A few months later, I had the opportunity to re-open my practice. It was still in the thick of Covid, but I managed to equip myself with the necessary precautions and convert a boutique hotel room into an independent hygiene clinic. Now that I also had this additional therapy - that could literally save people's lives, my goal was to build a collaborative team of health professionals and create a wellness component to a well- established spa in my area.

Sounds amazing for the workaholic, heart-centered businessperson I was deep down inside, maybe not for that new mother I had just become. I realized that even when I was home with this new, amazing baby I loved so much, my head was not. I love my kid, but I still love my career.

Luckily, God had another plan for me, yet again.

The collaboration was not quite coming together as expected, and among all the meetings and ideas floating around, I got pregnant again. I was going to have to put a pause on this plan for a few months. Like history rewriting itself, during that mere three-month postpartum time, I was notified that the hotel needed their room back as hospitality was reemerging. I did not have the time to commit, or the confidence, for the future we once hoped for, so I decided to move on.

Speaking of confidence, my confidence in my dream continued to grow despite these unsuccessful ventures. When you realize that life goes on, that you survive, that it's not actually that bad, you get more comfortable taking chances. I saw this drawback as a positive thing, rather than a story without a good ending!

I accepted that change is inevitable, and I was grateful for everything I had because I didn't have any regrets. Luckily my mindset was strong, because while I was considering my options of where and how I would now return to the workforce, I ended up losing childcare when new government subsidies rolled out and closed many small daycare facilities. I pondered and prayed for an answer, how was I going to provide for my family and still keep a piece of the person I was and wanted to be? Faith and gratitude kept me going, knowing there will always be something to enjoy - either my time with my kids, my time at a job, or time building an empire. I was able to accept whatever outcome came. Don't get me wrong, I hoped for certain outcomes over others, and the thought that *"I love my kids, but...."* cycled through my mind again.

Deep down, I knew there was an answer that would benefit me and my family. I just had to let it happen. I had after all, went from being homeless and working lots of minimum wage jobs, to becoming a supervisor in a casino, going from a professional healthcare provider, to becoming the president of the Canadian Dental Hygienists Association, while undertaking to the hardest task ever- becoming a parent! I just had to follow my intuition and act on any opportunities that were aligned with my passion, because I could never have predicted this life I have now.

I learned that for some tasks, we may never feel ready to undertake, and trust that knowing the route is not the only way to get to our destination. This was the point where I truly embodied that I would be okay with whatever outcome I ended up with, as long as my kids were healthy!

So, I continue each day, thanking God for the smallest (or sometimes *biggest*) things that filled each day. And I kept coming back to the one message all parents of teenagers and adults would say - *"Enjoy this time because it goes by so fast!"*

I hope you build the confidence to follow your heart, while enjoying the time you have, because that's the only thing you can't get back. And when it comes to *"loving your kids, but.....,"* your life will be full of disastrous moments that become the funny stories you will look back at and laugh about - like the tantrum they experienced when you peeled their banana for them, cut their sandwich the wrong way, fed their *"stuffy"* the wrong pretend food, or the times when they insisted they didn't need to pee, but as soon as you buckle them up or get their entire snow suit on, it's an emergency because they really **need** to pee, maybe it's remembering the fifteen minutes you spent in the grocery store bathroom while they sang and asked three hundred questions before they were done pooping! Whatever it was for you that made you think *"I love my kids...but,"* I hope you take this time now to reminisce on how much you love them, how it wasn't always easy, but to realize how much they changed or saved you.

If you happen to be a new mom reading this, I hope that it helps you become more present with family while you engage in the necessary self-care to allow you to show up your best!

A Mother's Prayer

"When I don't understand the child You gave me, comfort me and remind me that You are near."

By Prophetess Tolisha Suggs

Lord, here I am needing You as the foundation of my parenthood. I can't get this right without You. When I'm lost, lead me with divine direction. When I don't understand the child You gave me, comfort me and remind me that You are near. I can't do this alone. I've tried it my way, and now I'm desperate for You. So today, I give back to You the child You entrusted to me. I've wanted to be the superhero in their life, but today, I put down that cape and ask that You be their guide. Let them know I love them but that You love them more.

Lord, I ask You to disrupt every plan of the enemy and make every crooked place straight. Soften their heart, clear their eyes, and open their ears so they may see, hear, and understand the purpose You spoke over their life before I ever carried them in my womb. Let Your light outshine every darkness and may the things of this world lose their grip on them. Let them not be influenced by the world—but become influencers for Your Kingdom. I come against every assignment sent to harm them and declare it returned to sender, in the mighty name of Jesus.

Bless them. Redeem them. Protect them like only You can. In Jesus' name, Amen.

Petals Affirmation

"I am doing the best I can—
And that is more than enough."

By Dr. Tiesha N. Bryant

I am healed.

I am whole.

I am held.

I am loved.

I am love.

I am grace wrapped in strength.

I am softness anchored in truth.

I am learning.

I am growing.

I am doing the best I can—

And that is more than enough.

I am imperfectly perfect.

Not flawless… but divinely chosen.

Not always sure… but always showing up.

I am my child's safe place.

Their soft landing.

Their first home.

I honor my journey.

I release the shame.

I forgive myself for what I didn't know.

And I celebrate the woman I'm becoming.

I am not just a mother.

I am a miracle.

I am legacy.

I am love in motion.

I am whole.

And I am still blooming.

About the Curator

Dr. Tiesha N. Bryant, affectionately known as *The Parent Healer*, is a powerhouse of purpose, healing, and transparency. Born and raised in Pittsview, Alabama, she is a Licensed Master Social Worker (LMSW), emotional wellness coach, author, speaker, and certified global leader. She also serves as the co-host of *The Mom Panel* podcast, where real moms share raw truths and wisdom across cultures and life stages.

A teen mom at just 13, Dr. Bryant's motherhood journey has spanned every layer—joy, grief, bonus parenting, and becoming an empty nester at 33. She knows what it feels like to be judged, to rise against statistics, and to bloom in spite of brokenness. Her personal story is not just one of survival but of deep spiritual growth and legacy-building. She is the proud founder of both a nonprofit and a coaching and consulting business that empower families, youth, and women to heal, grow, and thrive.

Petals of Love: Chronicles of the Imperfectly Perfect Mother was curated from Dr. Bryant's heart—a sacred offering to mothers everywhere who have lived through "the in-between." This anthology is a space where vulnerability meets strength, and where every mother's unique journey is honored. Through her work, Dr. Bryant reminds women that healing is possible, purpose is real, and even the most difficult soil can produce the most beautiful flowers. Like the lotus, she continues to rise—soft, strong, and rooted in divine purpose.

Petals of Resources

Dr. Tiesha N. Bryant, LMSW| The Parent Healer|
info@resilientfamilywellness.com| www.tieshanbryant.com| Pittsview,
AL

Robyn Whitworth | The Original Elevated Mother|
Robyn@rrwsupportnetwork.org | www.evelatedmotherexperirjce.com|
Idaho Falls, ID

Jill Lerman| Play & Parenting Coach & Early Childhood Educator|
jill@jillybeansnyc.com| www.jillybeansnyc.com| Jersey City, NJ

Jacqueline Nole De Godbout | Podcaster|
btdubswithjackie@gmail.com | www.btdubswithjackie.com | Quebec,
Canada

Tiffany Ludwicki, Myofunctional Therapist | Mind Body Mouth |
tiffany@mindbodymouth.net | www.mindbodymouth.net | Newfound-
land, CA

Cristina P Simmons MS, OTR| The Trauma Alchemist|
info@cristinapsimmons.com| https://cristinapsimmons.com/| Central
FL

Chassidy Grady, Enrolled Agent| Tax & Biz Finance Expert|
Info@gradytaxplus.com | https://www.gradytaxplus.com| Magnolia,
TX

Trina Washington-Hawkins|
https://www.facebook.com/trina.washingtonhaw- kins/
https://www.instagram.com/trinawashingtonhawkins/

Alyssa Jenice Williams
DefineHer Founder • Elevation Coach | alyssajenice@definehermove-
ment.com | www.definehermovement.com | Atlanta, GA

Dr. Shalonda "Treasure" Williams-Lynard| The Nspirational Treasure|
Spiritsoulistic Coach & Spiritual Advisor|
www.thenspirationaltreasure.com | www.ko-fi.com/nspirationaltreasure

www.ingramcontent.com/pod-product-compliance
Lightning Source LLC
Chambersburg PA
CBHW051203120626
46547CB00012B/1184